The Word of S

The Word of Science

*The Religious and Social Thought of
C. A. Coulson*

David and Eileen Hawkin

EPWORTH PRESS

British Library Cataloguing in Publication Data

Hawkin, David J. (David John), 1944–
The word of science.
1. Religion. Relations with science. Relations
between science and religion. Theories of Coulson, C.
A. (Charles Alfred), 1900–
I. Title.   II. Hawkin, Eileen
215′.092′4

ISBN 0–7162–0462–2

First published 1989
by Epworth Press
Room 195, 1 Central Buildings, Westminster
London SW1H 9NR

Phototypeset by The Spartan Press Ltd,
Lymington, Hants
and printed in Great Britain by
Richard Clay Ltd, Bungay, Suffolk.

To Ben F. Meyer

magister et amicus

Contents

Acknowledgments   ix

Introduction   xi

1 Charles Alfred Coulson   1

2 Faith and the Challenge of Science   7
    1. The Modern Picture of the Universe   7
    2. Coulson's Views on Science and Creation   10
    3. The Question of Evolution   15

3 The Relationship between Science and Religion   23
    1. The Problem and Some Warnings   24
    2. The Scientific Method   33
    3. Reality and Reductionism   38
    4. Science as a Religious Activity   43

4 Science and Society   49
    1. Science and Change   49
    2. Science and the Future of Society   52
    3. Science, Nationalism and War   56
    4. The Real Value of Science   59

5 Responsibility in a Scientific Age   62
    1. The Scientific Task   62
    2. Responsibility, Science, and the Human Prospect   69

6 Coulson in the Contemporary Context   76
    1. The Need for Intellectual Responsibility   76
    2. The Need for Social Responsibility   80
    3 A Final Question   85

Appendix A
  Modern Cosmology and Some of its Implications   87

Appendix B
  Coulson's Pacifism   92

Appendix C
  Coulson's Non-Scientific Writings and Lectures   97

Abbreviations   105

Notes   107

Bibliography   121

Index   125

Acknowledgments

We wish to express our gratitude to Mrs Eileen Coulson for permission to publish extracts from the Coulson manuscript collection deposited in the Bodleian Library, Oxford. We are also grateful to the Keeper of Western Manuscripts at the Bodleian for permission to use the Coulson manuscripts and to the staff in the modern papers reading room for their courteous assistance.

Oxford University Press kindly granted permission to use material from *Christianity in an Age of Science* and *Science and Christian Belief*.

Some of the initial research on this book was made possible by grants from the Social Sciences and Humanities Research Council of Canada, Strategic Grants Division, and the Vice-President's Research Fund, Memorial University of Newfoundland.

Introduction

This book is not intended to be a biography of Charles
A. Coulson (1910–1974), although his life in itself would be a
fascinating study. What we are attempting here is an exposition of his writings on religion, science and society. He is best
known for his scientific publications which earned him
election as a Fellow of the Royal Society in 1950. But he
believed in the significance of his non-scientific writings
which focussed on the relationship between science and
religion and the effects of science on society. He wrote many
articles on these topics along with several books and a number
of pamphlets. Only two of his books, *Science and Christian
Belief* and *Science, Technology and the Christian*, reached a wide
audience. In our exposition we will draw attention to some of
his lesser known writings, especially those on responsibility.

There is a development in Coulson's thought. His early
writings on science and religion focussed on the relationship
between the two. In *Science and Christian Belief*, for example,
he discussed the common features which unite the universe of
discourse of science with that of religion. But over the years he
expanded his discussion more and more to include the moral
issues which arise from the impact of science on society. This
is seen clearly in his *Science, Technology and the Christian.*
Towards the end of his life he came to see that responsibility
was one of the great issues in the modern world. This is
exemplified in his little book, *Responsibility*.

Our treatment of Coulson's thought follows this development. Chapter 1 is a brief introduction to Coulson the man. In
chapter 2 we deal with some of the specific challenges to
religion posed by science, paying particular attention to the

issues of creation and evolution. Chapter 3 deals with the relationship between science and religion in general and concludes by focussing on a central theme in Coulson's thought: the idea that science is a religious activity. This is a seminal idea from which his thoughts on responsibility grow. The role of science in society and the importance of responsibility are discussed in chapters 4 and 5. Chapter 6 attempts to show the significance of some of Coulson's ideas for us today.

Chapter One

Charles Alfred Coulson

No treatment of Charles Coulson's thought on science and religion can ignore the man himself, for his writings express what he was: a scientist and a committed Christian for whom science and faith were inextricably united. He saw no dichotomy between science and religion, rather they were both expressions of a desire to understand reality. Through his radio broadcasts, public lectures, addresses and preaching, he tried to impart to a wide audience an understanding of the nature of science and its implications for the modern world. When a daily newspaper referred to him as a 'professor of theological physics' it was inadvertently stating a deep truth about him, for his life expressed the integration of his professional and religious beliefs in a remarkable way.[1]

Charles Alfred Coulson was born on 13 December 1910 in Dudley, Worcestershire. He was the elder of twin boys and he and his brother John were the only children. Before her marriage his mother had been headmistress of Tipton school. She encouraged her sons' early intellectual development at home where Charles learned to conquer long multiplication at the age of three. His father was principal of Dudley Technical College and was active in the Methodist Church. Although their mother was an Anglican, the boys were brought up as Methodists in the tradition of their father. Charles referred to the influence of his father in the dedication of his book *Science and Christian Belief*: 'To the memory of my father who first showed me the unity of science and faith'. When Charles was nine years old the family moved to Bristol after his father's appointment as H.M. Inspector of Technical Colleges for South-East England. Charles received good schooling there and was awarded a scholarship to Clifton College which he attended as a day-boy. In 1928 he went up to Trinity College, Cambridge, on an open scholarship in mathematics.

In his second year as an undergraduate at Cambridge Coulson joined one of the Methodist 'Groups' set up by Harold Beales, the minister of Wesley Church.[2] He later said that his first weeks in the Group were the most wonderful of his life. Although a member of the church up to this point, his interest had been 'perfunctory'. But after joining the Group he experienced God in an intensely personal way for the first time. This religious experience was to sustain him for the rest of his life. When Beales left Cambridge it was Coulson who supplied much of the inspirational guidance for the Groups. There are many who attest to his care and concern during this period, and there is no doubt that for Coulson himself his work in the Methodist Student Society, largely through the Groups, was a very big part of his life in Cambridge.

Because Coulson devoted so much time to religious and humanitarian work while he was in Cambridge, his father became concerned that he was neglecting his studies. But he need not have worried. His son had a tremendous capacity for work, and took a first in three parts of the Cambridge tripos, Mathematics Parts I (1929) and II (1930) and Physics Part II (1932). He was very fortunate as an undergraduate for he was able to hear lectures by such great scientists as Rutherford, J. J. Thompson, and Eddington, and he learned his mathematics from people like Hardy and Cunningham. After graduating he worked on his doctorate under Professor J. E. Lennard-Jones, who held the first, and for many years the only, chair of theoretical chemistry in Britain. Upon completion of this degree he was awarded a Trinity College Research Fellowship. During the period of the fellowship he worked with his close friend Douglas Lea on the influence of radiation on bacteria.

Coulson's interests were truly comprehensive and wide-ranging for he straddled the areas of mathematics, physics, chemistry and biology.[3] These Cambridge years set a pattern for his life-work in which he applied mathematical methods to more and more complex atomic and molecular structures in physics and chemistry. But he did not become a reclusive academic; besides his religious and humanitarian work he captained Cambridge University at chess, played cricket and tennis, and was an accomplished pianist.

In 1938, at the end of his Cambridge years, Coulson married Eileen Burrett, whom he had met there while she was training as a teacher at Homerton College. Before their marriage in Trinity College Chapel, Eileen had spent four years teaching in Leeds. Theirs was to prove a very happy relationship, her support and companionship being a major factor in his success and achievements. They eventually had four children: Andrew (1944), Martin (1947), Janet (1950), and Wendy (1952).

Both Charles and Eileen were very interested in the ecumenical movement. Eileen was an Anglican but she was to become a very active member of the Methodist Church. Charles regularly attended services at Trinity College Chapel but felt that he could not be in full fellowship with the other worshippers there unless he were a communicant member of the Church of England. This, together with his intended marriage to Eileen, prompted him to request of the Bishop of Ely that he might be confirmed in the Church of England. The Bishop was doubtful about the wisdom of trying to be both an Anglican and a Methodist at the same time, but Charles was not easily dissuaded. The Bishop acceded to his request in the end and confirmed him as a member of the Church of England.

Immediately after their marriage the Coulsons moved to Dundee where Charles had obtained a post as lecturer in mathematics at University College, then part of St Andrews University. The Second World War came soon afterwards. Coulson had publicly declared himself a pacifist in 1932, and he now applied for conscientious objector status, which was granted. His teaching load at the university increased as a result of the war, and he found himself lecturing in mathematics, physics and chemistry. But despite his heavy teaching load, he found time to write many scientific papers and an important scientific text-book. He began using quantum theory to investigate chemical problems in molecular structure. His work in this area turned out to be very significant and made him well known.

After the war Coulson moved to Oxford, where he was lecturer in mathematics at University College and ICI Fellow in Chemistry at the Physical Chemical Laboratory. He continued to make contributions in the area of molecular bonding. In 1947 he was appointed Professor of Theoretical Physics at King's College London, where he worked with his customary zeal at building up a new department. In recognition of his scientific achievements he was elected a Fellow of the Royal Society in 1950.

But Coulson did not like living in London, especially after his department moved to an underground building and his office did not have a window to the outside. He was a tall, lean man who loved the outdoors. He was passionately fond of camping, hiking and especially mountain climbing. He and Eileen went climbing at every opportunity. He was known as a colourful character, given to wearing old clothes and thick-soled walking shoes, bereft of all polish. His strong, dynamic personality coupled with his six foot four inch frame was rather overpowering for some people, but he was generally viewed as a warm, cheerful and optimistic person.

The Coulsons were quite pleased to return to Oxford when Charles took on the appointment as Rouse Ball Professor of Mathematics and Fellow of Wadham College in 1952. He was to remain in this post for twenty years. His reputation as a scientist was international, and he was invited to give lectures and talks in all parts of the world, including most European countries, the USA, Japan, Israel, Australia, Malaya, India, and East Africa. In 1955, he established a summer school in theoretical chemistry which was to become a model for similar schools elsewhere. By the end of his life he had published over 350 scientific papers and written four best-selling scientific text-books.[4] His graduate students, many of whom also became famous in their own right, came from all over the world. His research groups were truly international in composition for Coulson believed that science had an important role to play in uniting the peoples of the world.

This professional activity, which would have been more

than enough for most people, was only part of Coulson's life. He found time for religious, humanitarian and pacifist causes as well. He contributed to Methodism both as a much sought-after lay preacher and as the Vice-President of the Methodist Conference in 1959–60 (the highest post a layman may hold). His continued interest in ecumenism is evidenced by his membership in the Central Committee of the World Council of Churches from 1962 to 1968. He also devoted attention to the educational and developmental problems of the Third World. Before the war he and others in the Methodist Groups were very much aware of the general poverty and unemployment at home and concerned with doing something to help. After the war this same sort of concern was directed towards the international scene. Coulson was a member of both the United Kingdom National Commission for UNESCO, and the Royal Society UNESCO Committee, as well as being chairman of Oxfam from 1965 to 1971. He was also senior treasurer of the Joint Action Committee Against Racial Intolerance (JACARI) from 1956 until the end of his life.[5] In the 1950s and 1960s he gave most of his public lectures on science and religion. These were generally endowed university lectures and the list of them is impressive.[6] But he did not restrict himself to working for important committees or speaking to select audiences. He was just as much at home before a small congregation in a village chapel. His influence was felt by young people as well, for he spoke at many a school prize-giving ceremony and sixth form conference.

His life was filled with honours and awards, and some of his honorary degrees show clearly that he was highly regarded for more than his work as a scientist. He was made a D. Litt. by Sheffield in 1969, and a Doctor of Divinity by the University of St Andrews in 1973. One thing that gave him a great deal of pleasure was having his essay, 'The Age of the Universe', used in an anthology of models of good English prose writing.

In 1972 Coulson achieved his long-term ambition of establishing a department of theoretical chemistry at Oxford and became its first professor. Unfortunately, however, his health had begun to fail. He had been operated on for cancer in

1970, but the prognosis was good and he seemed to recover. However, by the autumn of 1973 the tumour had reappeared and treatment did not prove successful. The end of his life was typical of the way he had lived: having been told at the beginning of January that there was no hope of recovery, he faced the end with courage and peace of mind, supported by his Christian convictions. He put his affairs in order, dictating some eighty letters in three days. He then gradually became weaker and died in his sleep, at home, on 7 January 1974.

Upon his death tributes poured in from all over the world. He had touched countless lives through his professional, humanitarian, and religious activities, and he will not be forgotten by those who knew him. His scientific text-books and writings have met with due appreciation, but his writings on science and religion have reached a much wider audience. These have, moreover, shown a remarkable resilience to the passage of time, and still have a great deal to contribute to the contemporary debate about science and religion. It is the purpose of this book to explore that contribution.

Chapter Two

Faith and the Challenge of Science

1. The Modern Picture of the Universe

Our modern picture of the universe is quite different from that of classical antiquity. Aristotle thought of the earth as a stationary sphere around which the sun, moon and stars moved in circular orbits. The astronomer Ptolemy (second century AD) adapted and developed Aristotle's views into a complete cosmological system in which the earth stood at the centre of the universe. Ptolemy's system was adopted by the Christian church, which thought it quite compatible with its own doctrine of creation. The Bible describes how God created the world in six days, his final creation being humans who were given 'dominion' over all the earth (Gen. 1.28). This was also in accord with Aristotle's thought which gave human beings the primary place in the world scheme. Through its endorsement of the Ptolemaic system the Christian church wed itself to Aristotelian cosmology for over a thousand years.

In 1543, however, a Polish monk named Nicholas Copernicus published *De Revolutionibus Orbium Coelestium*, a book which proposed a quite different cosmological model. He suggested that it was actually the sun, not the earth, which was stationary.[1] The earth and the other planets in fact orbited around the sun. It was a revolutionary idea. Some simply dismissed it as absurd. Martin Luther, for example, described the idea as 'the over-witty notion of a fool who wished to turn topsy-turvy the whole art of astronomy'. But others took the idea more seriously, and during the next century people such as Galileo Galilei and Johannes Kepler studied the movement of the planets and on the basis of their observations concluded that Copernicus was right: the earth did orbit around the sun. (Copernicus was wrong, of course, in thinking that the sun itself was stationary.) Their ideas were not well received by those in the Roman Church hierarchy, whose authority had already been seriously eroded by the Protestant reformers. They saw the ideas of such as Galileo as a further challenge to their understanding of the faith. Galileo for his part argued that the Bible was not a scientific text-book and what it said about creation was to be interpreted allegorically. But he failed to win the day and was told in 1616 never to support publicly the ideas of Copernicus.

A few years later Galileo thought that the climate of opinion in the Vatican had changed, and was led in 1632 to publish *Dialogo dei Massimi Sistemi*, a book in which he repudiated the notion of an earth-centred universe. The work received widespread attention — too much for the church authorities, who subjected Galileo to the Inquisition and made him disavow his ideas. He was placed under house arrest and died in 1642. But his ideas did not die with him, and they sounded the death knell for the Aristotelian/Ptolemaic cosmological system and signalled the dawn of a new era in the thinking about the nature of the universe.

Whilst the church dithered and dallied over whether to embrace the new ideas on cosmology, the flower of scientific thought burst into full bloom during the seventeenth century. The pinnacle of scientific achievement of this period was reached with the publication in 1687 of Isaac Newton's *Philosophiae Naturalis Principia Mathematica*, widely regarded as the most important scientific work ever written. In it Newton put forward his theory of gravity to explain how bodies moved in space and time, and in doing so set the scientific agenda for the next two centuries. It was not until 1905 that Newtonian physics was superseded with the publication of Albert Einstein's paper on relativity. Relativity signalled an even more dramatic change in the way we think about the universe, revolutionizing our concepts of space and time and divorcing modern cosmology completely from the Aristotelian/Ptolemaic system to which the church had for so long been wedded.

What are the elements of modern cosmology which differentiate it so markedly from the older Ptolemaic model? In the first place, modern cosmology points to a universe of enormous size. Far from being the centre of the universe our earth is a tiny planet, orbiting a perfectly ordinary medium-sized star in just one of countless galaxies. The universe is so big that it is virtually beyond imagining – when people speak of the earth being like a grain of sand on a mile long stretch of beach it just adds to the sheer incomprehensibility of it all. Moreover, the universe is not only staggeringly big, it is also amazingly old. It is thought to be approximately 10–15,000 million years old, while the age of our own planet earth is around 5,000 million years. This is rather different from Augustine's estimate for the age of the earth as 5,000 years and Archbishop Ussher's (more precise) estimate that God created the world in 4004 BC![2] There was, moreover, a great period of time before the human race itself came into being. Most scientists estimate the human race to be about one million years old. This is equivalent to about six seconds if we think of the age of the universe as a whole day. These ideas do not suggest any great significance for humans in the overall scheme of things![3]

This picture of a universe of immense size and great age poses a genuine challenge to Christian thinking. It is impossible to reconcile such a picture with a literal interpretation of the biblical account of creation in which God created the world in six days and gave human beings pride of place in it. There are now very few Christians, however, who take the biblical account of creation literally. Galileo may have lost his own personal battle with the church authorities, but his view that the Bible is not a scientific text-book has won out in the end. Few Christians would want to defend the scientific accuracy of the biblical account of creation. Where the Bible and science are seen to conflict on the facts of creation, science carries the day.

To say that the biblical account of creation is not to be taken literally does not, however, divest it of its significance. The doctrine of creation is a central one in Christianity: the Bible begins with God's creation of the world and it is featured prominently in the creeds. If the biblical account of creation is not to be taken literally, just what is its significance for today? Has Christianity anything at all to say about creation or must it surrender all claims about it to science? Coulson was acutely aware of such questions and faced squarely the issues arising from them. It is instructive for all Christians to see how he dealt with them.

2. *Coulson's Views on Science and Creation*

Coulson believed that Chistianity did have something meaningful to say about creation without denying the validity or significance of the discoveries of science. He therefore sought to facilitate a dialogue between science and Christianity. Now for Coulson dialogue was not an argument; it was, moreover, 'seldom a debate and never an acrimonious struggle'.[4] When two parties enter into dialogue the right of each to speak openly and freely is presupposed and it is accepted that any truth claims which are made have a partial character. The goal is mutual understanding, even if mutual agreement is not always possible. It was in this spirit that Coulson wrote about the relationship of science to Christianity and in particular the claims of each about creation.

In setting creation at the beginning of its Bible and its creeds, says Coulson, Christianity is giving a framework within which the life of humankind may be understood. It asserts that the physical world was made by God and for some purpose. Coulson never tires of making this point. Christianity is not an otherworldly piety. It says not only that human actions can be understood by reference to God, but also that the world itself in which humans live – 'the very stage on which our little act is performed' – was designed by him. Coulson puts this in an aphorism which he often repeated: 'God not only directs the play, he built the theatre.'

But there is another reason for Christians to take the physical world seriously. At the centre of the Christian religion is the incarnation. In the incarnation God not only concerned himself with human affairs, he entered a physical world. This, Coulson maintains, gives the world itself a sacramental value.[5] He quotes approvingly a statement from

Hort's Gifford lectures, *The Way, the Truth and the Life*, that 'the Gospel itself can never be fully known till Nature as well as Man is fully known. Every addition to truth becomes a fresh opportunity for adoration.'

Coulson thus believes that the Christian religion is fundamentally concerned with the physical world and this requires it to come to terms with science. God created the world, therefore understanding it will lead to a deeper understanding of God himself. Thus the scientist could (and should) contribute to speech about God – to 'theology'. Theology is not the exclusive preserve of clerics or professional theologians. The scientific contribution is, however, couched in different language from that of traditional theological discourse. To gloss over this fact does a disservice to both science and Christianity. One must listen intently and with an open mind to what both Christianity and science have to say.

In his writings on science and creation Coulson's major concern was to engender an atmosphere where mutual respect and understanding would prevail over bigotry and ignorance. He admits that there have been Christians who have been 'unintelligent in their use of the Bible', but also says that some scientists have been equally unintelligent in their use of science. His basic starting point in his discussion of the issues is that 'God wants Christians to use their heads.' If we use our heads we will find that God is revealed in many different ways. Science, by throwing light on the origin and development of the world, throws light on the nature of God. To deny that science can tell us anything about God is to deny that we can know God through the physical world, which in effect is to deny the full significance of the creation story. It is to set the spiritual over against the material, something which Coulson considers to be gravely mistaken. (Although Coulson never refers to the Gnostics, his own argument here is very similar to that used by the Early Church Fathers in their refutation of Gnosticism.) To argue that the material and the spiritual should not be severed in the Christian life is not, of course, to deny the importance of individual experience of God. It is rather to assert that God reveals himself not only in the spiritual life of the individual believer, but also in nature. A

Christianity which fails to recognize this is 'enfeebled and impoverished'.[6]

It was in this frame of mind that Coulson looked for the truths contained within the creation story. He argued that in fact there were three central truths which were quite compatible with science. The first of these truths was that 'God made everything':

> It was *His* mind, *His* restless creative energy that formed the starry clusters in the sky and conceived the very light by which we see them. 'In the beginning God' . . . There were six days of creation, as if to emphasize the colossal nature, the enormity (if once you let yourself think about it) of all that God did when he fashioned the length and breadth and depth and height of this strange panorama.[7]

So the first truth is that it was God, not humans, who made the world.

The second truth revealed in the creation story is that there is a purpose in this world, and that it is God's purpose, and his alone:

> For there were six days of creation, and not one: and did not man himself come upon the scene when all other created things were already there? The universe in which we live may be mysterious, but it is not haphazard or accidental. We may rightly use the word evolution to describe this process, provided only that we do not mean some sort of automatic process which, once started, simply had to go on to its inevitable conclusion. The universe is not a clock which God, the clockmaker, wound up at the beginning, and which is now ticking away in some monotonous meaninglessness. Genesis says that if only we can see big enough – and Heaven help us, for most of us can't – we can trace in what we call the Order of Nature, the working out of an almost unbelievably grand purpose.[8]

The last of the three truths which Coulson sees in the creation story is that God's purpose is incomplete without humankind. The pattern of the universe needed humanity to complete it.[9] This truth was one on which Coulson frequently

elaborated. God gave humankind a *magisterium* over all creatures; this was a gift, not a right, and carried with it a 'solemn
responsibility to use it properly'. We shall examine how
important this theme of responsibility is in Coulson's
thought in a later chapter; it suffices here to note that his idea
of responsibility is inextricably tied to his understanding of
the *magisterium* which was given to humankind in Genesis.
When Adam and Eve acted irresponsibly they were expelled
from the Garden, and thus through the 'sweat of their brows'
human beings relearned their relationship to the material
universe, and in the fulness of time saw 'the material and the
spiritual intermingle, and all things be summed up in Christ,
who is both creator and redeemer'.[10] In saying this, of
course, Coulson goes beyond the idea of creation founded in
the Old Testament and finds its true meaning in the New.

These three truths found in the biblical account of creation
are also to be found in the story told by the scientist. Coulson
argues first that the Christian belief that God created the
heavens and the earth is similar to that of the scientist who
says, 'I believe that there is something beyond me, over
against me, separate from me, which I can study, which I
must accept and to whose laws I must conform.' Coulson
was aware, of course, that there were scientists who, if asked
whether they believed in God, would reply 'No'. But he was
very impressed by the earnest way scientists pursued their
ideas. He often spoke of scientists who made fun of their
apparatus and working conditions, but who never made fun
of the truth they were investigating. Coulson became accus-
tomed to calling this reverence for truth a response to the
'wholly other'. This is reminiscent of Rudolph Otto who
uses the same vocabulary: the scientist and the Christian
believer both respond to the numinous, the awe-ful. 'Without this belief that there really is something outside himself,
and outside all other human beings, and yet which can be
known to him and to others, all the patient work of the men
of science would be foolish babbling.'[11] Thus, despite the
claims of some scientists to the contrary, the scientist's
attitude of mind is 'essentially religious'. As Einstein had
said:

You will hardly find one among the profounder sort of scientific minds without peculiar religious feelings of his own . . . His religious feeling takes the form of rapturous amazement at the harmony of the natural law . . . this feeling is the guiding principle of his life and work. It is beyond question akin to that which has possessed the religious geniuses of all ages.[12]

The second truth which Coulson finds in the biblical account of creation is that the universe exhibits a meaningful pattern. Now the whole scientific enterprise is predicated on discovering patterns in the things observed. The scientist begins his inquiry with the belief that there is an order to be discovered and science has, as a consequence, been very successful in finding such patterns. The scientific method would be simply arbitrary and yield meaningless results if there were not in fact an order in the universe which could be unveiled and communicated. To quote Einstein again:

God, who creates and is nature, may be very difficult to understand, but he is not arbitrary or malicious.[13]

This brings us to the third truth, that the pattern of nature is incomplete without humanity. This, says Coulson, is what not only Genesis but also the scientist says when he reflects upon what he is doing. For it is the human mind that devises the scientist's experiment, observes it, and interprets the evidence which comes from it. Some scientists have maintained that science is most objective when the human element is reduced to an absolute minimum. But in his lectures to a SCM group at Manchester in 1956 Coulson pointed out that this was a 'dangerous half-truth':

For if by 'cutting himself out of the picture' we mean a willingness to accept truth even if it conflicts with his personal predilections, and to 'follow into whatever abyss or onto whatever height', then we are right. This is because, as we have seen, every scientist must be in a creaturely relationship to the universe which he studies: it is God's universe, and not his. But if we mean the human element plays no part in science, we are wholly wrong. It is central to the whole business. For example, the universe has almost certainly existed for a very long time before the human race began; suns had set and moons had waxed and waned, but no one had seen either the beauty or the pattern. There would have been no scientists without human beings to become scientists. There would have been no revelation of the nature of God within the natural order without human minds to be aware of this order and study it. It is in this sense that the order of nature finds its completion only in man.[14]

The doctrine of creation is, then, an integral part of the Christian tradition, and its insights are in fact deepened by the discoveries of modern science. For Coulson a Christian doctrine of creation 'finds not only an echo, but a bodying forth, in the conclusions of modern scientists'.[15]

3. The Question of Evolution

We have seen how for Coulson the physical world – what he often called 'the world of things' – was important for the Christian. He was against making too sharp a distinction between the sacred and the secular. He often argued that laymen had an important contribution to make to Christian self-understanding because they placed more value on the world of 'things'. Clerics and those in religious orders tended to focus their attention on spiritual matters. The difference between the two is mirrored quite nicely in the Russian language where the word for priest means a 'spiritual man' or 'otherworldly man' and the word for layman means 'man of the world'. Coulson did not believe that this kind of sharp divorce between the sacred and the secular was fundamentally Christian. He supported his view, as we have noted, not only through his interpretation of the biblical account of creation, but also by pointing to the fact that Christianity was an incarnational faith. God himself entered the physical arena which humans inhabit – the world of hot and cold, light and darkness, pleasure and pain – and thus sanctified it.

One of the implications, then, of Coulson's understanding of Christianity is that the physical world, the world of things, has value in and of itself. Another implication is that the world has its own history, independent of humankind, a fact which Coulson thought in no way compromised his assertion that the creation of human beings completed God's plan. In fact Coulson often asserted that there was movement, change, progress, development, evolution in the world of nature.

The word 'evolution' inevitably conjures up the spectre of Charles Darwin, a figure who continues to be a haunting presence for many Christians. Coulson frequently referred to the initial controversy over Darwin's theory as a 'storm in a Victorian teacup' (a description he borrowed from Charles Raven). But he never imperiously dismissed the controversy as being too silly to deal with. Rather, when appropriate occasions arose, he would carefully explain the issues and recount the events surrounding the reception of Darwin's book. The single event which captured the issues most dramatically took place a year after the publication of *On the Origin of Species*, at the British Association Meeting in Oxford. The publication of *The Origin* had aroused the interest of biologists everywhere, and they came to Oxford in June 1860 to debate the questions Darwin's work had raised. Darwin himself did not attend the meeting because of ill health, but his position was ably defended by Joseph Hooker and the well-known combatant, T. H. Huxley. Arguing against Darwin's theory was the Bishop of Oxford, 'Soapy Sam' Wilberforce. Coulson tells us that Wilberforce claimed he got his nickname because he was constantly getting into hot water and coming out clean. On this occasion, however, he got scalded. For in his argument against Darwin and his followers he resorted to personal invective and scorn, and lost the debate.

Wilberforce's position was a simple one – if the theory of evolution were true, the Christian estimate of humankind would be wrong:

Mr Darwin writes as a Christian, and we doubt not that he is one . . . We therefore pray him to consider well the grounds on which we brand his speculations . . . First, then, he declares that he applies this scheme of natural selection to man himself, as well as to the animals around him . . . Now we must say at once, and openly, that such a notion is absolutely incompatible, not only with the word of God on the subject, but with the moral and spiritual condition of man . . . Man's derived supremacy over the earth; man's gift of reason; man's free will and responsibility; man's fall and man's redemption . . . are all equally and utterly irreconcilable with the degrading notion of the brute origin of him who was created in the image of God, and redeemed by his eternal Son.[16]

In recounting this story Coulson always bemoaned the fact that Wilberforce received such strong support from some Christians (although, it should be noted, not from all). The simplest refutation of Wilberforce and his followers is to say that Genesis is not a scientific text-book, which it obviously is not. But Coulson was not content with only this argument. He saw the story of evolution as 'setting before us a pattern of quite incredible wonder'. Evolution pointed to God, not away from him. Moreover, in Genesis, if we read perceptively, there is a sense of movement, development, progress and change. Is not creation spread over six days, rather than in one great fiat? Ultimately, however, Coulson did not think that the 'storm in a Victorian teacup' was about the first chapters of Genesis. He thought that the real issue was the autonomy of science. And now that science had won its autonomy, its right to interpret the world according to its own agenda and criteria, the dispute at Oxford over a hundred years ago seems somewhat passé. The theory of evolution did not destroy Christianity as Wilberforce feared, but, thanks to people like Coulson, it has in fact contributed to its deeper understanding.

The ideas of evolution, and the findings of science in general, show that there is a pattern to the world. As an undergraduate in Cambridge in 1931 Coulson attended James Jeans' Rede lecture on *The Mysterious Universe*, and had been struck by Jeans' suggestive picture of humans stumbling by mistake into a universe which was not designed for life and which to all appearances is either indifferent or even totally hostile to it. Coulson had wondered if it really was the sum total of human destiny 'to cling to a fragment of a grain of sand until we are frozen off, to spend our tiny hour on our tiny stage with the knowledge that our aspirations are all doomed to final frustration and that our achievements must perish as though we had never been'. But he could not accept such a picture. And even a religious sceptic like Fred Hoyle had come to the conclusion that 'life was not a meaningless accident'.[17]

Christians, however, see more than a pattern in nature: they see God working through it. It was Charles Kingsley who said that the theory of evolution gave one a choice of either believing in a God who behaved arbitrarily, or believing in one who was active and present in things. Coulson echoed this sentiment in his Owen Evans lectures when he spoke of the 'divine immanence in creation'. There is, of course, a danger in using science in an effort to substantiate such a statement, and Coulson was well aware of this. In the same lecture he spoke of how Lecomte du Nouy had used scientific evidence in an unfortunate way to conclude that the emergence of life was so improbable that it must have come about by a direct act of God.[18] Du Nouy was a biologist who was interested in the possibility that a series of atoms of hydrogen and carbon, oxygen and nitrogen, flying at random through the gas of the atmosphere, might meet and collide together in such shape and pattern that the simplest bit of biological material could be formed. He used various devices to estimate what the probability was, and he concluded that it was incredibly small.[19] It was at this point that he unwisely drew the moral that the emergence of life was so improbable that only an act of God could explain it. It was unwise because it was an unscientific conclusion based on scientific postulates. Du Nouy had strayed from the field of physics into metaphysics. Moreover, within a few years other scientists were able to show experimentally that du Nouy had erred in his probability calculations.

Du Nouy was not the only scientist to be singled out by Coulson as an example of someone who strayed inadmissibly from physics into metaphysics. He had a great admiration for Teilhard de Chardin, but in painting his complex picture of all nature evolving towards consciousness Teilhard had referred to the 'within' and the 'without', the 'within' apparently applying to even single molecules. But what exactly does this mean? As Coulson wryly commented:

I have studied molecules for 30 years or more. I should be exceedingly surprised if I could say anything about the 'within'. I don't think it has any meaning to talk about it. One of the temptations which scientists are prone to is to lapse from strict physics into metaphysics, and pass off what are metaphysical views as if they were scientific ones.[20]

Drawing non-scientific conclusions from scientific observations may also lead to views different from those of du Nouy and Teilhard, as in the claim that the living and changing universe is wasteful, arbitrary, and without purpose. Such a claim is just as open to criticism as the claims of du Nouy and Teilhard. It is one thing, for example, to observe scientifically the death of large numbers of creatures such as the fairy shrimp, and quite another to declare that this shows purposeless destruction. And indeed, in the case of the fairy shrimp what appears to be an example of the arbitrary and brutal ways of nature seems less so when the full facts are known. The fairy shrimp (a rare creature with many natural enemies) inhabits small, shallow ponds. Every summer these ponds dry up, and the shrimps die.[21] A pointless tragedy? Such a judgment would take us beyond science, but what closer observation tells us is that when the pond dries it kills off not only the fairy shrimp but also its natural enemies. The eggs of the fairy shrimp, however, are adapted to survive, and when they later hatch they have no natural enemies with which to contend, and so the chances of the survival of the species are enhanced. The moral is clear: we may observe nature's ways, but we must be careful about drawing conclusions which go beyond simple empirical observation. Similarly, Christians have to acknowledge that when they say they see a pattern in nature, and that this is God working through it, they have made a statement which is not strictly scientific. This does not mean that they cannot make such statements, but it does mean that they should be aware of the pitfalls involved in moving unwittingly from empirical observation to metaphysical statements.[22]

Evolution implies not only change in the order of nature, but also change in the way human beings function within that order. We are more and more able not only to control our environment, but also our own biological destiny. Coulson was writing before genetic engineering became a major focal point of scientific inquiry, but he nevertheless anticipated the kind of discussion it might provoke. There are increasing numbers of people today who are worried about the kind of power which the new techniques in genetic engineering are giving scientists and who suggest government restrictions on the kind of research which should be permitted. A similar suggestion had been made in Coulson's time by the distinguished Australian Nobel prize winner Sir MacFarland Burnet. Coulson's response to this idea of restricting scientific research and knowledge was quite unequivocal. As a Christian he believed that all knowledge ultimately came from God. We have to learn to live with new knowledge, no matter how dangerous this seems, for we have been given the privilege of sharing in the creative work of God himself and we must accept the responsibility which comes with that privilege:

> If there are those who say to us [that] the power of manipulating the human race is such that you cry halt, then I think that the Christian community must rise and say, 'To talk like that is to blaspheme against the Holy Spirit.' I have spoken strongly because I feel strongly.[23]

Darwin himself had wondered whether human beings could cope with the consequences of their own evolution. Have we evolved too quickly for our own good?[24] Coulson did not think so, although he did recognize the great challenges which new developments would bring. He thought of there being three great stages in human history. The first, 'when Adam dug and Eve span', was the age of unaided human effort. The second was the industrial age, in which machines began to replace human toil. We are now entering the third stage, the age of cybernetics. In the industrial age machines did our work for us. In the cybernetic age machines will do our thinking.[25] Coulson died before microcomputers revolutionized modern life, but he anticipated well their effects. He foresaw that societies would have great difficulty adapting to a computerized world. For if the industrial age had devalued human work and created great social tensions through the loss of, for example, employment, how much more would be the tensions brought about by machines which devalued human thinking! But Coulson did not believe the problems created by the arrival of computers were insurmountable. Indeed, there were advantages to having machines which did so many things better than human beings. What he did not foresee, and really could not have anticipated, was that highly sophisticated computers combined with a global telecommunications system would create an entirely new phenomenon – a technology which, because it is greater than the sum of its parts, becomes autonomous. This is a point to which we shall have to return in our concluding assessment of Coulson's thought.

Coulson's optimism about the future was rooted in his Christian faith, a fact he openly acknowledged:

> Those who do not believe that this is God's world, that therefore behind all the flux of events there can be traced some kind of purpose greater than ourselves, have every reason to be afraid. But those who believe that it is God's world, that when you break into the nucleus of an atom you release the energy which he put there millions of years before the first human foot trod this planet's surface, those people can give something to a time like the present . . .[26]

To the objection that by accepting the secularity of the world the Christian is in effect handing it over to humanism, Coulson replied that as this is God's world, there would eventually come a moment when secular inquiry would ask questions that reveal the essentially spiritual character of secular life. Christians, meanwhile, have to play their part in enlightening the world. This, however, is no easy task. In the modern world it is no longer sufficient simply to call for a 'decision for Christ'. The complexity of today's world has made the Christian vocation more subtle than that. Coulson used to tell a humorous story, now become very familiar, about an Englishman visiting Ireland who got lost, and upon finding one of the locals asked him how to get to Roscommon.

'Oh, is it to Roscommon you be wanting to go?'

'Yes, it is,' said the Englishman.

'Shure; by Patrick, it is this that I tell you, if it was to
Roscommon that I wanted to go, it would not be from here
that I would be starting.'

This is to illustrate that whilst the final goal for Christians
may still be relatively clear, the point from which they are
starting – this complex, modern, scientific world in which we
live – is not. Coulson devoted much of his life to the search for
the understanding of this starting point. He also elucidated
several principles to help guide us to where we should be
going. These principles are firmly rooted in his understanding
of creation and evolution. But before we examine these
principles in greater detail, we will turn to a wider examina-
tion of his discussion of the relationship between science and
religion.

Chapter Three

The Relationship between Science and Religion

Charles Coulson was both an eminent scientist and a committed Christian. In his life science and religion did not keep to separate compartments, nor did they war with each other. They attained a unity which he tried to explain and express to other people. He was not attempting to be a philosopher of either religion or science, but wanted to contribute in his own way to a dialogue between the two. To the Christian who was not a scientist he tried to communicate that there was nothing to fear from science but rather a lot for which to be grateful. He described science as a 'religious activity' and by doing so no doubt caught the attention of many religious people who might otherwise have missed the discussion. To scientists he wanted to impart the understanding that science alone gives but a partial grasp of reality, albeit an important and essential one. He wanted both scientists and theologians to 'take off their blinkers' and each recognize the insights that the other had to offer.

His basic ideas were presented in the first two of his non-scientific publications, 'The Christian Religion and Contemporary Science'[1] and 'The Place of Science as a Cohesive Force in Modern Society'.[2] He continued to expand on the major tenets of his argument in several important invitational lectures which were subsequently published: the Riddell Memorial Lectures published as *Christianity in the Age of Science* in 1953; the 1954 Rede Lecture published as *Science and Religion – a Changing Relationship*; the 1954 John Calvin McNair Lectures[3] published as *Science and Christian Belief* and the 1958 Eddington Memorial Lecture published as *Science and the Idea of God*. The best known of these is probably *Science and Christian Belief*. This book received wide acclaim and won the Lecomte du Nouy Award for most effectively emphasizing the relationship between science and religion. In it Coulson wished to show not only the propriety of holding Christian beliefs in a scientific age, but also that science is essentially a religious activity. A lot of what he had to say anticipated issues that have been taken up in a contemporary debate spearheaded by people such as John Polkinghorne and Arthur Peacocke. Like Coulson, these men also are scientists by training. We will follow Coulson's thought as he attempted to bring science and religion closer together, and highlight some of the points he made which speak to contemporary issues.

1. *The Problem and Some Warnings*

There is a common perception that science and religion conflict and that science effectively discredits religion. This is a relatively modern idea and when Coulson dealt with it he always put it in some kind of historical perspective. What we think of as modern science actually developed within the Christian tradition. Some people even view it as a fruit of Christianity, but at the very least 'it may safely be asserted that it can never spontaneously grow up in regions where the ruling principle of the Universe is believed to be either capricious or hostile'.[4] The Royal Society, which in England has been very important in the growth of science, was founded in 1645 and had among its first members two bishops, John Wilkens and Seth Ward, a doctor of divinity, John Wallis, and other deeply religious men such as Robert Boyle, John Ray, Christopher Wren and Isaac Newton. In its second charter the Royal Society directed its Fellows to work for the 'glory of God the creator, and the advantage of the human race'. It was not until the nineteenth century that the word 'scientist' was coined – and by the end of that century large-scale professional science was taking over from the 'amateurs'. In the space of two hundred years science had undergone tremendous growth. The rate at which it grew did not allow for the gradual adapting of older views to accommodate the new.

Traditional processes were replaced by 'new, improved' scientific ones, and of necessity, knowledge began to break up into many separate disciplines. The age of specialization was upon us.

As science grew so did the tension between science and religion. In the nineteenth century the notion of conflict came to the forefront of public attention with the controversy over Darwin's theory of evolution. Science had reached the stage where it needed its autonomy from religion. It wanted to go its own way without having to use God as a premise. Questions that could be phrased in scientific language were demanding scientific answers, not metaphysical ones. With this call for autonomy came the fear that science would destroy religion. This fear is understandable in the light of some of the claims that have been made and continue to be made in the name of science. Waddington said: 'Science itself, and so far as I can see, only science by itself, unadulterated with any contrary ideal, is able to provide a way of life which is firstly self-consistent and harmonious, and secondly is free for the exercise of that objective reason upon which our civilization depends.'[5] As Sir Richard Gregory put it in his own epitaph:

My grandfather preached the gospel of Christ
My father preached the gospel of socialism
I preach the gospel of science.[6]

Science came to be perceived as the most powerful, vital and cohesive force in society.

The story of Christianity's response to this tremendous challenge is not an inspirational one. A lot of mistakes have been made. One common fault is described by Coulson as the disease of 'hardening of the arteries of Christian thinking'.[7] This is simply the denial of new knowledge out of fear of its implications. It was the problem he saw with Wilberforce's reaction to Darwin's theory of evolution, and it can be seen today within sects on the fringes of Christianity who deny some of the findings of science. It is the clinging to an outmoded and discredited world-view rather than a reverence for tradition. As a response to the challenge of science it can only be regarded as misguided, doing justice to neither science nor religion.

But it was not just a matter of science and religion denouncing each other. Many scientists were also Christians, and it was with their attempts to resolve the tension resulting from this that Coulson particularly tried to deal. A common approach taken by scientists was to impose some sort of separation between science and religion. There were those who viewed them as two distinct worlds, completely separate from each other. 'It was said of Michael Faraday that when he turned from his prayers to his laboratory he forgot his religion; and when he closed the door of his laboratory to leave it he forgot his science.'[8] This may not have been quite fair to Faraday,[9] but it exemplifies one kind of attitude that prevailed. Coulson thought it a very dangerous one, leading as it must to a kind of moral schizophrenia. This is even more true today. In an age of nuclear-pumped lasers, hydrogen bombs and genetic engineering, if a scientist believes that what he does in his laboratory has nothing to do with his life outside of it, we have a sure recipe for disaster.

Another type of separation involved a division of experience into two autonomous but contiguous regions, like adjoining countries, with science governing whatever it could and religion handling the rest. In this view there are certain things which only science can explain, and other things which only religion can explain. One obvious problem with this is that, as science grows and extends its boundaries, religion is squeezed out. Yet examples of this approach abound and continue to arise. We can recognize it when Newton wrote to the Master of Trinity College, Cambridge, explaining how his theory of universal gravitation applied to 'phenomena as apparently distinct as the fall of an apple to the ground and the length of the lunar month'; but regarding the rotation of planets round their axes, he went on to say: 'The diurnal rotation of the planets could not be derived from gravity, but required a Divine arm to impress it upon them.'[10] It was not long before the 'Divine arm' ceased to be needed here. In a similar vein Descartes concluded that, since he could not find a function for the pineal gland, it must be the residence of the soul. But the function of the pineal gland was found and, presumably, the soul could not reside there any longer.

Coulson saw it as imperative that Christians should not resort to introducing a 'God of the Gaps' – that is, trying to find God in those areas which science had so far failed to explain. He quotes Henry Drummond as saying: 'There are reverent minds who ceaselessly scan the fields of nature and the books of science in search of gaps – gaps which they fill up with God. As if God lived in gaps!'[11] Coulson's view of the matter was that 'When we come to the scientifically unknown, our correct policy is not to rejoice because we have found God: it is to become better scientists.'[12] And even more pointedly he said: 'A scientist who has to appeal to God to get his results right, or who introduces God as the repository of his ignorance when the results are not clearly explicable, is no true scientist'.[13]

Coulson did both Christianity and science a great service by drawing attention to gaps. He put us in a better position to be aware of the mistakes that can be made and the traps into which both science and religion can fall. He showed us also the importance of paying close attention to the history of science. Yet, despite our awareness of gaps and the ease with which we can spot them after they have been filled in, new gaps seem to be notoriously difficult to recognize. When confronted with them even the giants have been deceived – we would hesitate to say of either Newton or Descartes that he was 'no true scientist'. Today this idea of the 'God of the Gaps' has found a permanent place in the literature on science and religion. Credit for defining the concept and exposing the problems with it rightly goes to Coulson. But perhaps, and somewhat unfortunately, his fame for this idea has overshadowed other fine contributions he had to make.

Science seems to have found itself at a genuine boundary with the realization through quantum theory that there is a fundamental unknowability at the very heart of matter. Judged by everyday standards, the quantum world is very strange indeed. It is a world subject to Heisenberg's uncertainty principle and dominated by statistical probabilities. It cannot be encompassed by everyday notions and frequently defies common sense. The uncertainty principle says that we cannot know simultaneously both the position and momentum of an elementary particle; that is, as John Polkinghorne puts it, we cannot know at the same time both where an electron is and what it is doing.[14] In our familiar everyday world we can make statements such as 'At 3 a.m. the car was heading north at the intersection travelling at ninety miles an hour.' The quantum world does not allow for such a combination of knowledge about its inhabitants. The more precisely we try to determine where an electron is, the less can we say about how fast it is going. Our usual reasoning is not reliable either. For example, if we are told that Johnny is playing, and is either in the backyard or at the park, then we can conclude that we will find Johnny playing in the backyard or we will find him playing at the park. Such everyday common sense is an application of what is called the distributive law of logic. In the quantum world, however, this law no longer holds – a parallel statement would not permit us to draw a similar conclusion. Fortunately, Johnny is not an electron.

John Polkinghorne explains that the 'peculiarities of quantum mechanics' created a need for modification in classical logic:

> It arises because of a characteristic quantum possibility (called 'superposition') which allows, for example, a particle to be in a state where it is neither definitely 'here' nor definitely 'there' but has certain probabilities of being found either 'here' or 'there'. This is a middle term of a type undreamed of by Aristotle.[15]

In the world of Newtonian physics the laws of classical logic apply. It is a predictable world of causes and effects. This determinism is missing from the quantum world. Our knowledge of quantum events is statistical, depending on large numbers, while individual events are unpredictable. This leaves an irreducible element of chance at the very heart of matter. Some scientists found this idea hard to accept. Einstein, in particular, could not believe that God would, in his words, 'play dice with the cosmos'. He made persistent, but unsuccessful, attempts to find something wrong with the uncertainty principle.[16] There were others who accepted the uncertainty principle but took the view that the unpredictability might be due to causes which are inaccessible to us.[17]

> On this view, the exact time at which every unstable atom decayed would in fact be fully determined, but by a mechanism of which we are unaware. In a sample of such atoms the different hidden settings of these internal clocks would produce the sort of statistical distribution that quantum theory predicted. But all the time there would be this comforting regularity beneath the surface; the sound of rattling dice would have been banished from fundamental physics.[18]

For very good reasons, however, most scientists do not hold this view. They generally agree that individual quantum events are 'uncaused' – that the unpredictability of the quantum world is in the very nature of things.[19]

Oddly enough this same uncertainty and reliance on probabilities which can be so distasteful to some people has almost irresistible appeal for others. For those who had difficulty grappling with the problem of how God could act in a world that is completely governed by scientific laws, this introduction of uncertainty and mystery was a welcome relief. During Coulson's time, W. A. Whitehouse expressed it this way:

> [I] am attracted by the fact that scientific explanations and predictions rest now on the 'law of great numbers'; that the fundamental physical laws are statistical and not exact in the popular sense. Why this should be so is an interesting matter for speculation. It may provide a sufficient room for manoeuvre, beneath the observable regular processes, for the personal care of God to be actively exercised.[20]

William G. Pollard, a physicist and theologian, accepted that chance had a fundamental role to play in modern physics, and he was drawn to the idea of God acting in the world at the sub-atomic level. In this way God could influence events without being seen to break scientific laws, for the laws govern aggregate effects only and leave individual outcomes free to be determined as necessary. He explored this idea in his book *Chance and Providence* in 1958.[21] We do not know how Coulson responded to Pollard's arguments in particular, but we can see that he was not favourably disposed towards such arguments in general:

> A God who is obliged to conceal His actions of providence so that we cannot see Him, a God who hides His presence in Nature behind the law of large numbers, is a God for whom I have no use; He is a God who leaves Nature still unexplained, while He sneaks in through the loopholes, cheating both us and Nature with His disguised 'room for manoeuvre'.[22]

Coulson went into some detail about Heisenberg's uncertainty principle because of what he saw as its wrong use as a basis for metaphysical arguments. The statement of the principle in terms of position and momentum conjures up a picture of a world inhabited by tiny particles, like billiard balls. Those who are so inclined are then free to imagine a God who influences events on a large scale by somehow adjusting the behaviour of these little particles. To dispel this particular image, Coulson pointed out that the uncertainty principle is really only about the limits to the precision of physical measurement. It does not tell us in any way how to picture the quantum world. In fact, two different models are necessary to describe behaviour there – we need both a particle model and a wave model. The limits on measurement apply to both models:

> [The] uncertainty principle only talks about the results of measurement. It says nothing about the validity or otherwise of the model which we are using . . . An electron is not a particle, though it may be good enough for many purposes to treat it as if it were. An electron is not a wave, though again for certain other purposes it may be convenient to treat it as if it were. This means that the electron does not lead us to the gateway of religion: it leads us to think a little more deeply about our science, and to modify

our fundamental concepts to bring them into line with the increasing variety of our experiments.[23]

We have seen that Coulson would not accept the idea of God living in gaps or working under cover of large numbers. There is yet another popular way to get to religion from science – through what is known as arguments from design. This type of argument features prominently in a revival of natural theology that has been going on in recent times. The idea is, basically, that there is an order, constancy and intelligibility in nature that points to God, or at least to the probability of God.[24] The discussion has been carried out mostly by scientists of religious conviction and is marked by a great deal of controversy. For example, Teilhard de Chardin argued that evolution pointed towards a truly grand design which would issue in a consummation of purpose for humankind.[25] More recently, however, we have Jacques Monod, a biologist like Teilhard, arguing in his book, *Chance and Necessity*,[26] that evolution shows quite clearly that there is no purpose – rather chance is the basic constituent of the human predicament. Monod attracted a lot of response. A particularly cogent one came from a statistician David J. Bartholomew in 1984 with his book called *God of Chance*.[27] In it Bartholomew acknowledged that his own interest in the relation between science and religion went back to hearing Coulson speak on various occasions in the 1950s.

Coulson sounded a lot of warnings about arguments from design, although he did not believe that discourse in natural theology was unfruitful. He regarded the use of any specific phenomenon to support the argument as perilous and cited the well-known example, used by Charles Raven,[28] of the parasitism of the common cuckoo to illustrate this:

> On first inquiry it seems that a sequence of at least five distinct events must occur, each of which is outside the run of normal behaviour and structure, if the performance is to be successful . . . Each of these events is necessary for the whole process, yet each by itself is useless. The odds against such a series, if it be regarded as pure chance – the result of some set of synchronized mutation among the genes – must

be astronomically small. Is there not here a strong argument from Design?[29]

Coulson showed that this argument is, in fact, suspect. By reference to the book on evolution by David Lack[30] he was able to point out that not all of the five essential events are quite so essential as had been thought. In particular, not all species of cuckoo have abnormally small eggs, nor does the colour of the eggs necessarily match that of the host, and in many species the young cuckoo does not eject the other young from the nest. We find ourselves back in a 'God of the Gaps' situation with the gap beginning to close and God being squeezed out.

The appeal to particular examples to support the argument from design is fraught with difficulties. This has been shown in Richard Dawkins' recent, highly acclaimed book, *The Blind Watchmaker*. Dawkins borrows the image of the watchmaker in his book title from the famous illustration by William Paley. Paley suggested that if we examined a watch found on the ground, and knew nothing of its origin or purpose, because of its complexity and design we would still have to conclude that it had a maker – that there was, in fact, a watchmaker. Similarly, argued Paley, the complexity and mystery of the world we live in suggests a maker or designer – God. Dawkins argues that 'natural selection is the blind watchmaker, blind because it does not see ahead, does not plan consequences, has no purpose in view'. The 'living results of natural selection' give 'the appearance of design as if by a master watchmaker' but this is, in fact, an 'illusion'.[31] Dawkins argues that the evidence of evolution reveals a universe without design.

While it is open to question whether Dawkins succeeds in showing this to be the case, there is no doubt that he does show the folly of appealing to particular examples to support the argument from design. He would have found no disagreement from Coulson on this point. The argument from general principles is, however, somewhat different. The idea that there is an 'order and constancy' in nature is the very bedrock upon which science is founded. The conviction that the world is rational and intelligible is behind all scientific endeavour. Coulson used arguments like these himself, but as to their being a direct pointer to God – he again took a very cautionary stance.

One warning he gave was that we must be careful not to equate a sense of order with God himself. But more fundamentally, the fact that humans discern order in the world may be saying more about the way the human mind operates than about the real nature of the world. Coulson borrowed a well-known parable of Eddington's to illustrate this: an ichthyologist went fishing in the sea to find out all about sea-creatures and then made two broad generalizations from his catch – that no sea-creature is less than two inches long, and that all sea-creatures have gills. These conclusions seem to be about fish but actually say more about the size of the mesh he was using and the construction of his net. What we have here is selective information, and 'as with the ichthyologist's net, the only information which our brains can ever receive must come to them in this selective fashion . . . We had better be careful lest what we may believe to be the glory of God should turn out to be nothing other than the glory of man.'[32] James Jeans used to say that God was a pure mathematician, but Coulson suggested that this God might really be James Jeans in disguise.

Of course, Coulson was not saying that there is no order in nature except what we have put there ourselves. He was sounding his usual warnings about how careful we must be when using arguments of this type. It was not a question of abandoning discourse in natural theology, rather of approaching it carefully and critically. Both Eddington and Faraday had thought that ultimately the findings of science were immaterial for Christian faith, or, as Eddington put it, 'irrelevant to the assurance for which we hunger'.[33] For Coulson, and others who insist on the unity of human experience, 'this wholesale rejection of Natural Theology will not help us very much'.[34] While the scientist cannot look to the substance of his inquiry to find God, Coulson believed that valuable insights were to be gained by looking to the manner of his inquiry. Consequently, he had much to say about the scientific method.

2. *The Scientific Method*

A popular notion about science is that it is a system of proven laws based solely on undisputable facts. Advertisers use the phrase 'it has been scientifically proved' with a view to having their claims accepted without question – you just do not argue with the facts. People are encouraged in this attitude by the great public success which science has enjoyed. Coulson saw this reverent approach to facts as quite unwarranted and considered it dangerous. His particular concern was with the way in which it contributed to the dichotomy between science and religion. But he also recognized that it gave science a rather dull, plodding image which did not attract creative young people. Therefore, he set out in many of his writings to show that science was not such a creature of fact and logic as was commonly supposed. His delightful article 'Fact and Fiction in Physics' was devoted exclusively to putting facts in their proper place.[35] As a renowned scientist he was in an ideal position to tell us how science is really done. He explained this in a clear and simple way with generous use of examples and quotations from other scientists. We will indicate here some of his main points.

Facts for their own sake are of little interest to a scientist. The interest lies in the use to which they may be put. Neither are facts just there. They arise out of experiments which are done for a reason – usually the hope or suspicion that something will happen. Facts are also somewhat limited by the thought-forms of the time in which we live because it is rather difficult to see something for which one is not looking. Then there are some areas of science in which observations are inextricably bound up with the use of instruments, for example astronomy and atomic physics. A reading on a dial might be a fact, but it is hardly a very useful one in itself. It must be interpreted. The fact which emerges upon interpretation is really a blend of theory and observation, often open to dispute. It is no longer a fact of the cold, hard variety. In the words of Eddington: 'There are no purely observational facts about the Heavenly Bodies.'[36]

Whole areas of science are based on concepts that cannot be considered factual at all. 'We know that atoms and electrons are of the very life blood of physics. We dare not abandon them. Yet they live with us not so much as facts but as our own brain children, about whose reality and parentage it behoves us not to ask too many questions.'[37] Yet scientists are prepared to act on these concepts with results as impressive as the atomic bomb. 'Arthur Compton described the whole of the atomic bomb project . . . as one colossal act of faith.'[38]

When it comes to the status of those 'proven' laws that make up the body of science, Coulson tells us that scientific laws are not facts, nor should they be thought of as having been proved. A scientific law 'is essentially a description of the results of observations'.[39] It represents an attempt to find a pattern that makes sense of our experiences and observations. Also 'there is no ultimate and final proof of any scientific theory that may be proposed, but only the possibility of disproof when a clear prediction is not fulfilled'.[40] The reasoning involved is from particular examples to general rules. This inductive logic can be very skilful, but no finite number of examples can ever prove a rule – that is, show it will be true in all possible of an infinite number of cases. A rule can be proved false, however, using the safety of deductive logic by exhibiting one counter-example. So whence comes our faith in scientific laws if they have not been 'proved'?

Scientific laws are indeed accepted as true without logical, rigorous proof, yet they are certainly not pure fiction. A law is acceptable when it is 'without internal contradiction, and is able to grow, either by the prediction of new phenomena or the absorption of old ones'.[41] At the heart of scientific truth is a developing, growing quality which scientists recognize and accept. Even publishers of scientific text-books expect them to need revisions and corrections within a few years. Part of the verification that scientific laws are not pure fiction lies in the instrumental use of scientific models 'both to predict the future and in varying degrees to control the environment'.[42]

Since scientific laws are not a matter of deduction we must wonder how scientists come up with their laws in the first place? It is generally agreed that this is essentially a creative activity in which a key ingredient is imagination. Coulson quoted many scientists on this point, among them Max Planck: 'New ideas are not generated by deduction, but by a creative imagination, for science is a creative work of art.'[43]

But this imagination is not just wild and unbridled. Conceivably there could be many theories, essentially different from each other, which would all fit the evidence that is available in a particular situation. Scientists must make choices about which path to pursue and judgments as to what is worthwhile research. In these judgments they are guided by considerations of simplicity and beauty. Einstein is quoted as saying: 'Our experience up to date justifies us in feeling that in Nature there is actuated the idea of mathematical simplicity.'[44] Scientists can actually have more faith in a law by virtue of its simplicity than by the actual empirical evidence for it. Coulson tells that after Clerk Maxwell applied rigorous tests to Ohm's law – a law that had been established by experiment and not deduced from other principles – he made the comment that 'the mode in which it has borne this test not only warrants our entire reliance on its accuracy, but encourages us to believe that the simplicity of an empirical law may be an argument for its exactness'.[45]

So we see that facts themselves are not science; rather they are the servants of science. Scientists must go beyond the facts. On this Coulson quoted T. H. Huxley: 'It is generally supposed that the scientist is under obligation never to go beyond the facts. But those who know anything about these matters are aware that a man who never goes beyond the facts very seldom gets even as far as that.'[46] An important part of the service that facts render is that they act as a 'trigger'. 'They set us going on a strange voyage where imagination, beauty and pattern are our signposts.'[47] The highest praise that can be given a scientific theory is that it is not merely true, but that it is also simple and beautiful.[48] Of course, in going on this strange voyage, science must never lose contact with reality. Here again facts perform a service, for the right fact can shoot down a beautiful theory that is on the wrong track. We cannot emphasize the simple and beautiful to the point of ignoring the true. Fortunately they all tend to go together.

In 1986, with his book *One World*, we find another scientist, John Polkinghorne, describing the scientific method for us. His description is much like Coulson's and his up-to-date examples make some of the points very sharply. He says that, to be acceptable, a scientific theory must be 'fruitful'. This is a beautifully descriptive word for what Coulson referred to as the ability to cope with old phenomena and predict new. He shows scientific truth in the same light as Coulson and describes the achievement of science as 'gaining a tightening grasp on actual reality'.[49]

Polkinghorne discusses the philosophical positions of positivism, idealism and realism and takes the time to place himself squarely in a camp he calls 'critical realist'. While Coulson did not stray from his purpose to debate with philosophers of science, he occasionally could not avoid confronting them. One would not dare call him a positivist after reading: 'Let the logical positivists roar and rant – that is the way science grows.'[50] Neither should he be labelled an idealist.[51] He insisted on, and explained, his belief that there really is an observed apart from the observer. There cannot be complete separation between the two but what the scientist does is to seek out 'the invariants of the combined system of observer-plus-observed . . . These invariants . . . are what we mean, scientifically, by reality.'[52] 'The whole edifice of science is too austere, too majestic, too successful and too compelling to be dismissed as nothing "but the baseless fabric of a vision".'[53]

If Coulson were to wear a philosophical label, he would probably be comfortable with that of 'critical realist'. It is a realist position in that it holds that our understanding of the world is dictated by the way things actually are. It is critical, rather than naïve on three counts: at any moment verisimilitude is all that can be claimed as science's achievement; everyday notions may prove insufficient to deal with regions remote from our experience; and the role of judgment cannot be discounted.[54] Coulson has shown himself in agreement with all these points and, no doubt in the company of a lot of other working scientists, could join the same camp as Polkinghorne.

One reason why scientists like Coulson and Polkinghorne felt it necessary to describe the scientific method is because most people are not aware of how much science has changed since the nineteenth century. It has become much less dogmatic about its ability to understand the world com-

pletely. The idea that science is totally without presuppositions – in particular contrast to religion which is supposed to
be full of them – is now recognized as untrue, and, in fact,
impossible to attain. Coulson acknowledged our debt to
people such as Polanyi and Whitehead for pointing out these
presuppositions. As John Polkinghorne described it, science
has been taken 'off the pedestal of rational invulnerability' and
placed in the 'arena of human discourse'.[55]

But, at the same time, science is being given credit of
another kind – it is being recognized as one of the great
movements of the human spirit. Coulson tells us that
J. B. Conant described 'the great conceptual theories of
modern science' as 'monuments to what the human spirit can
achieve'. He also referred to the historian, G. Sarton, who said
that the true humanist 'should know the life of science, as he
knows the life of art and religion'.[56] The scientist is now seen
to be much closer to the artist, poet and historian than was
previously thought. Many people will regard this change of
image as a definite improvement.

3. Reality and Reductionism

That there actually is a reality there to be grasped was never in
doubt for Coulson. And that there is but one reality, and not
two or many, was also never in question. He illustrated his
conception of this by using analogies drawn from personal
experience. However one may feel about the use of analogies,
they help a great deal in understanding the position of the
person who is offering them. One of Coulson's favourites
came from his experience of mountain climbing, especially in
Scotland.

A mountain is one reality. But to get to know it requires
seeing it from many different viewpoints – from different
directions, from far away and near, in different seasons and
different weathers. To 'know the Ben', for example, one
'must have been on the mountain, and have reached the top
not only along the gentle slope from the Youth Hostel in Glen
Nevis, but no less from the Mountaineering Club hut on the
other side'.[57] He has given us to understand that this other side
poses quite a challenge for even the experienced climber.

Another mountain he described is called Schiehallion. From the east, some distance away, it 'looks exactly like a huge pile of sugar' – a cone shape. But from the south, at the same distance, you can see quite a broad top on it.[58] So experience shows that with a mountain different viewpoints can yield different, and sometimes contradictory, descriptions. Yet some of the mountain's features will appear in more than one description, although perhaps with different degrees of centrality.

Just as there are many different views of a mountain, all of which are necessary if you wish really to know it, so too are there many different views of reality given to us through science, religion, art, poetry and so on. We can feel confident that they are not all describing different realities when we trace common features in their descriptions and notice similar insights that have been gained through different approaches. Some of the great truths of art, philosophy and religion have been expressed, in its own way, by science. For example, the 'brotherhood of man' is being revealed when science describes the desire and need for co-operation and communication among human beings.

The mountain is a powerful image for reality. It is there, it is one, and to be known it must be encountered – you must have been on the mountain. All viewpoints available must be given due consideration if we are to tighten our grasp of it. There is, however, an unfortunate aspect of this analogy that Coulson did not like. Without stretching it too far it was difficult to think of religion as anything but one view among many. This is not quite in keeping with the way in which a Christian sees the role of his religion. While Coulson was willing to classify a lot of theology as just a view, yet at the heart of Christianity there is a unique act of revelation. Coulson wanted to do justice to this as well.

A later analogy, which he developed fully in *Science and Christian Belief*, attempted to come to terms with the special claim of Christianity. It is drawn from his involvement with the building of an underground laboratory at King's College in London. He often had occasion to consult the architect's drawings which were of many different types. There were ground plans, elevations, and cross-sections; some had a lot of detail and others had very little. No one plan was exhaustive and none was superfluous. The plans were two-dimensional, yet it was possible to get some concept of the actual three-dimensional building by putting them together. You could not just superimpose one picture on another, but needed to build up a sort of 'stereoscopic vision' of the building from them, in the same way that our eyes gain for us a sense of perspective and solidity by seeing things slightly differently. In this analogy, Coulson let the plans of the building represent the different disciplines of science, history, art, and so on. But he was able to let religion have a unique role. It provided the 'act of reflection' which was needed to put together the partial views and build up something of the three-dimensional character of the building itself. This act of reflection represented a gaining of insight rather than just an addition to knowledge.[59]

We can see from Coulson's own analogies how vital for him was the concept of unity. There is but one reality. Yet it is mysterious and elusive and can only be grasped partially and in a piecemeal fashion. No one discipline has the whole truth about reality, nor even about any part of it. This strikes at the very heart of reductionism. Unfortunately, reductionist ideas come all too easily to scientists.[60] When it was believed that nature could be studied in a completely objective way, only one answer was expected to any question – the solution to nature's cryptogram, as Leibniz called it. Now that science has grown so vast, any one scientist must concentrate his gaze on a very small area, shutting out all else. It is easy for him to see nothing but what he is doing and conclude that his is the only view. Neither are scientists shy about expressing this. For example, Coulson quoted Sir Ernest Kellaway as saying, 'Only one description of the universe, or of any part of it, can be true'; and from Aldous Huxley: 'To talk about religion except in terms of human psychology, is an irrelevance.'[61]

Reductionist ideas must not be considered harmless:

Disaster can follow from a statement such as the one attributed to the American philosopher John Dewey, that with the advent of science 'morality is only an engineering issue', or the statement of the chairman of a united council of Christians and Jews: 'If 600 scientists working together in the early days of the war could solve the problem of the atomic bomb, then surely 600 scientists working together now could solve the problems of race relations.'[62]

Reductionist attitudes are very much in evidence in the world of business and industry. Coulson often warned about the prevalence of these ideas. For him, nothing could be more foolish than to accept just one picture and deny any others. Yet that is precisely what he saw being done continually in schemes for social management and industry. He summed up his warning thus:

> It amounts to this: that the concentration on 'one' frame-work of description, 'one' interpretation, to the exclusion of all others, must inevitably imply the impoverishment of our response to whatever situation confronts us; and is likely to lead us into the most hideous conclusions.[63]

A strong pointer away from reductionism can be seen within physics itself where dualism of description has become a way of life. For example, when it came to studying light some phenomena were best understood by thinking of it as composed of particles while other phenomena could only be described by thinking of it as a wave. This caused great controversy as to what light actually was, since such a duality was considered, at the very least, to be improper. But neither description would go away, and as they refused to be reconciled, scientists had to live with both of them – one at a time. It was the same thing with the electron. There are two models, and both are necessary in order to do justice to the phenomena. Each model is complete in itself and they are mutually exclusive. To try to have them both at once causes confusion; to have one without the other impoverishes.

Years of familiarity finally helped the physicists grow comfortable with this duality. Coulson said: 'Most of us have lived so long with this that we have grown used to it; and have come to see the great and liberating influence inherent in the

two modes of description.'[64] The idea attained full respect-
ability when Niels Bohr gave it a name. He called it the principle
of complementarity. (In the mathematical sense to be complementary also includes being mutually exclusive.) Science
progressed, not by insisting on knowing exactly what an
electron is, but by developing reliable models to describe and
predict its behaviour. Like Galileo they are leaving the 'hard'
questions for now and concentrating on those they think might
yield answers. Today it is only the non-scientist who dares to
ask, 'Exactly what is an electron?'

This idea of duality does not argue against the unity of reality
because the dualism is not seen to lie in the electron itself or in
light itself. It lies in our own language and concepts and models
which we must use in trying to understand them. If dual models
are necessary in describing an electron, how can we excuse
reliance on just one model when dealing with issues that involve
people and their societies and industries?

We have seen that Coulson was not one to use scientific
concepts in a metaphysical way, nor to sit by quietly when he
saw others doing it. But he saw no problem with calling for a
wider application of the principle of complementarity with all
its 'liberating influence'. That would be the application, not of a
concept, but of an attitude – the attitude of acceptance towards
seemingly contradictory aspects of a complex reality. He saw
some controversies being resolved – not by arguing conclu-
sively for one side or another – but by recognizing the two sides
as complementary aspects of the same situation. A problem
simply dissolves when it is amenable to this kind of treatment.

One controversy Coulson handled in this way was that of
whether the will is free or determined. He painted a vivid
picture of President Roosevelt agonizing over his decision
whether or not to declare war on Germany, and then the
historians coming along and explaining why the whole thing
was inevitable. He allowed that both viewpoints are correct.
From the point of view of the actor the will is free; from that of
the spectator it is determined:

> Free will is a concept, and determinism is also a concept. We
> introduce the concept of free will to make sense of the

experiences that we have, of fear and hesitancy and hope, when reflecting on the relation between our past and our future. And in the same way we introduce the concept of a determined will to relate significantly two elements from our own or someone else's past. There is no conflict of concepts. Each is valid in its proper context.[65]

He also thought that this idea could shed some light on the mind/matter controversy. But he considered this topic rather 'dangerous' and preferred to speak in the words of the psychologist, Sir Cyril Burt:

> Perhaps, after all, neither matter nor mind is wholly real; both material objects as we ordinarily conceive them, and what we call our minds, may turn out to be just superficial appearances, or (if you like) superficial interpretations of something that is neither purely physical nor yet purely mental – something whose pattern or structure we perhaps discover, but whose intrinsic nature we can never guess.[66]

Here we see mind and matter being described as different aspects of the same reality. The concept we use should depend upon the context. Coulson suggested that 'wisdom' consists in knowing which concepts to use in a given situation.

This mixing of concepts outside their proper context has been the source of a lot of the tension between science and religion. Problems that arise this way are more phantom than real, and honest attempts to solve them have often been misguided. The scientist who says he cannot find God with his telescope nor the soul with his microscope is right. These concepts do not belong to the framework of physics. To try to answer him by locating God at the end of his science or within its gaps does justice to neither science nor religion.

4. *Science as a Religious Activity*

Coulson was convinced that when it came to the relationship between science and religion, too much energy was going into answering the wrong sorts of questions and following false clues. He attempted to balance the picture by focussing on the common ground between the two. In fact, he went so far as to

describe science as a religious activity. Other areas of human
endeavour also share in the common features he pointed out.
He was well aware of this. But the main thrust of his argument
was that, in some very important ways, science did not stand
out as being different.

Some of the common ground between science and religion
is due to the way in which science grew up in a Christian
environment. Data from religion could be deliberately ex-
cluded from science, but basic attitudes and presuppositions of
a religious nature were carried along as it grew, even though
these may often have gone unrecognized.

> That common search for a common truth; that unexamined
> belief that facts are correlatable, i.e. stand in relation to one
> another and cohere in a scheme; that unprovable assump-
> tion that there is an 'order and constancy in Nature' . . . all
> of it is a legacy from religious conviction.[67]

No one would want to be rid of this legacy, however, for the
success of science has conferred a sort of validity on holding
these assumptions.

As for attitudes of mind, Coulson points out examples of
patience, humility, fair-mindedness, integrity, and co-operation. About these he says:

> [They] are the hallmarks of our tradition. And they force
> me to the conclusion that this tradition is ultimately based
> on, and derives its final sanction from, moral convictions
> which are often unrecognized, but none the less impera-
> tive.[68]

There is another similarity between science and religion in
that they are both attempts to make sense out of experience,
and try to do this by creating suitable concepts and models.
Both science and religion begin with experience – that is
primary. Science starts with its experiments and builds up its
models and concepts. But the concepts of science acquire
validity only in experience. Human experiences of a personal
religious type lead people to concepts as well, and these too
acquire their validity only in experience. On this point
Coulson liked to quote his friend, Alex Wood, a physicist,

who wrote, 'What I really feel is that Christ has verified Himself in my experience and He can do it in yours.'[69]

But there is a clear difference between the experiences of science and those of religion. The experiences of science can be shared with others. Experiments can be repeated and rational arguments can convince. Personal religious experiences, however, cannot be shared in this way. They cannot be made real to others through rational discourse.

> [In] religion there are concepts – a personal God, a redeeming power, the activity of the Holy Spirit – none of which can be said to be collectively and publicly knowable in any direct fasion; but a case can be made for introducing them since by no other means can we do justice to the feelings of awe and worship, of sin and of release which we experience in our lives and which we see also to be meaningful in the lives of others.[70]

A quality that we tend to associate mostly with religion, but which is also present in science, is a sense of revelation. It is associated with the process of discovery, and refers not to the information obtained but rather to the sense of illumination that can accompany discovery. Coulson liked the way Sir Lawrence Bragg expressed this:

> When one has sought long for the clue to a secret of nature, and is rewarded by grasping some part of the answer, it comes as a blinding flash of revelation: it comes as something new, more simple and at the same time more aesthetically satisfying than anything one could have created in one's own mind. This conviction is of something revealed, and not something imagined.[71]

Christianity also lays claim to a special revelation, but that is of a different nature and has no place in science.

The idea that science and Christianity share important common features has also been put forward by Arthur Peacocke. He noted that both science and religion had a communal quest for truth; in both a kind of humility was required; both appealed to experience; and both used models or analogies whilst recognizing their inadequacy.[72]

If we are willing to compare science with religion from the

point of view taken by Coulson and Peacocke, we have to conclude that there are a number of important similarities. But pointing out common features does not necessarily lead one to say that science is a religious activity. The activity aspect that Coulson saw as essentially religious is akin to the 'act of reflection' that he spoke of in his analogy of the building plans. He put it this way:

> It is in this reflective sense that I want to claim that all science is an essentially religious activity. To accept Nature as, in some senses, given; to receive the gift, and behave in a creaturely fashion towards it; to believe that it carries with it meaning and significance; and to seek, in reflection, what that meaning is – this surely is to act religiously.[73]

No doubt there are scientists who would baulk at having their activities described in these terms. But, as Coulson has shown, there are many others for whom this is indeed the correct picture. The very idea that science can be presented in this way by scientists should make an impression on Christians who have not given science its full due as a valid mode of God's revelation. They should realize that there are insights to be gained by listening to what science has to say – insights both unique and awesome, into nature, people, and God himself – that may not be obtainable in any other way. God is not so small that he must be fitted into or around science. Rather science is one of the ways in which God is mediated to us.

There is also a simpler sense in which Coulson wanted the concept of science as a religious activity to be understood. It was the sense intended by John Ray, the botanist, who called the pursuit of science an essentially religious activity in that it was 'a fit subject for a Sabbath day'.[74] Having seen science described as it has been by Coulson, a Christian would hardly be likely to disagree.

An important feature in all that Coulson had to say about science and Christianity is that the relationship has been a changing one. Science began as a child of Christianity, guided by it and doing its bidding. Then it developed into a rebellious adolescent demanding autonomy and believing it knew, or could know, everything. Now it is growing to a maturity and responsibility, no longer so dogmatic, and in important ways not unlike its parent. Christianity must now take seriously what science has to say, and where necessary enlarge its own concepts to incorporate these insights properly.

In Coulson's view some of the most important insights that science has to give us involve the relationship between nature and humanity. The great advances in astronomy have shown us that the universe does not revolve around humankind. It is so big and has been there so long that it must be important in its own right. We can no longer hold the eighteenth-century view that it is all there for our own pleasure and profit. Even the suggestion that this vast scale of time and size was a necessary prerequisite for the development of humans[75] does little to dampen our sense of awe when we are confronted with the marvellous ideas about the universe to be found in the popular books of scientists like Fred Hoyle and, more recently, Stephen Hawking.

Neither can we just acknowledge the marvels of the universe and allow that God must have his own reasons for wanting it, but then assume that it really has nothing to do with us – that we are somehow separate. The fact is we do not even get a special creation of our own. Theories about evolution have been busy finding our place in the scheme of things. There is no denying that nature was there first and we grew out of it.

There is also a sense in which atomic physics is showing how inextricably linked humans and nature really are. 'We have come to recognize that the act of measurement of any of the minute particles of our physical world so alters it that there ceases to be continuity between "before" and "after". Physicists like Heisenberg and Bohr have stressed how impossible it has now become to distinguish with precision between the observer and what he observes.'[76] Human beings and nature are intermingled. People grew out of nature and so are a reflection of it, yet the very laws of nature are human constructs, and in that way nature is a reflection of humanity. It becomes difficult to tell where one ends and the other begins. 'Von Weiszaecker has recently likened these two aspects of the relation between man and nature to the two semicircular arcs which together comprise a complete and closed circle, in which one cannot speak of a beginning or an end.'[77]

Within the great concepts of science, therefore, we can read the message that nature and humankind are not separate but are closely involved with each other. This infuses nature with a personal quality that must influence our attitudes and inform our views on a whole range of issues.

One important implication of this closeness is that any relationship between God and people must include nature as well. We cannot endow humankind with religious significance without also giving it to nature. This is in sympathy with an incarnational religion. Coulson said: '[We] begin to see, as in olden days we could not possibly have seen, how the Christian view of nature makes sense, albeit terrible and tragic and joyous. We can hardly be surprised now at the idea of an incarnation: no lesser involvement of God with His own handiwork can do justice to its relation to ourselves.'[78] In Christ 'we see in its plainest form the wretchedness and greatness of life, and are led to a new interpretation of the inner meaning of suffering and sacrifice'.[79]

Ideas like these have been expressed very beautifully by the philosopher Erazim Kohák when he deals with the problem of pain. He says that when humans realize that they are not the measure of all things, and neither are they alone, then they 'discern the humility of their place in the vastness of God's creation, [and] that creation and its God can share the pain. For Christians, the Cross symbolized that reality; confronted with it, the human is not freed of grief, but he is no longer alone to bear it. It is taken up, shared.'[80] Kohák goes on:

> That is the age-old wisdom of the book of Job . . . the zealous young Elihu offers the best that the rabbinic orthodoxy of his time had to offer . . . When God speaks, the framework is different. He speaks not of pain, but of the vastness of creation, of the gazelle in her mountain fastness and the mighty creature of the deep sea. God is not avoiding the issue. He is teaching Job the wisdom of bearing the pain that can neither be avoided nor abolished but can be shared when there is a whole living creation to absorb it.[81]

Chapter Four

Science and Society

1. *Science and Change*

Modern society is characterized by change. It is constantly undergoing dramatic and often unforeseen change. The countryside is rapidly disappearing as people move from large cities into smaller towns. These in turn eventually expand into larger conurbations. This urban sprawl together with the rapid improvement in communications has given rise to a society quite unlike that into which our great-grandparents were born. The rural community with its hard work and intimate relationships has given way to a fast-paced society dominated by cars and computers and a leisure culture which experiences much of life vicariously through television, radio and films. If we were able to take a Roman of the first century and transport him into the eighteenth, we would probably find that he would adapt fairly quickly to his new surroundings. But if we were to transport him into the twentieth century, he would probably fare very badly. The impersonal and rapid pace of urban life would be too removed from his own experience. Waddington puts it like this:

> Horace would have felt himself reasonably at home as a guest of Horace Walpole, and Catullus would have soon learned his way about among the sedan chairs, the patched-up beauties and flaring torches of London streets at night. But if the time translation had lasted for another two centuries they would have found themselves in the position of bewildered children, their daily life dominated by the

automobile, the telephone, the inexorable time-table of relationships with the innumerable people who form inescapable links in ever-ramifying chains of administrative arrangements without which the simplest necessities of life . . . cannot be carried on. For the common man, who had no privileged position but earned his living by his own labour, the change would have been even greater. The rural peasant or blacksmith of Roman times would find his modern counterpart, the urban industrial or clerical worker, as strange as a being of a different species.[1]

The entire history of the human race is, however, a history of change. Within the last four hundred years in particular there have been some dramatic changes in the history of the Western world. The religious renewal of the Reformation, the struggle for freedom in the French and American revolutions, and the economic and social upheavals of the industrial revolution have all been epochal changes. So what is the justification for claiming that the modern world is so different?

Coulson argued that one big difference is that in the modern world technology has become inextricably linked with science. This means that the changes of the modern era are qualitatively different from those of previous revolutionary eras. In arguing this Coulson is laying no claim to orginality. Others have argued the same point, both before and after him. The case has been especially well put by the profound Canadian thinker, George Grant.[2] Grant claims that in our society there is a radically new relationship between making and knowing (technology and science) which changes both activities. We are now dominated by a mode of technological thinking which has spawned a monolithic way of looking at things. There is no way left to criticize the assumptions of technology without appearing to be irrationally opposed to the facts and benefits of scientific discovery.

Coulson's account of the fusion of knowing and making was not as philosophical as Grant's. Nor was he as pessimistic as Grant about our ability to think through the problems created by modern scientific progress. Coulson was a scientist and he dealt with the issues in a straightforward way using examples from the history of science. One of the examples Coulson used to illustrate the new relationship between making and knowing was the Dupont Chemical Company, which is one of the largest in the world and yet it had been in existence a hundred years before it began to combine its chemical research with technological applications. Another example came from his own family history. His grandfather had been an inventor who had been awarded a number of medals for his work. But he had no scientific training. His inventions came entirely from old-fashioned common sense and practical experience.. He would have been ill at ease in today's world, where engineers and technicians must have scientific training to be taken seriously. In 1785 James Watt and Matthew Boulton, the instrument maker turned engineer and the industrialist, were elected to the Royal Society. But they were the exception rather than the rule. It is only in the modern era that it has been commonplace to expect a scientist to combine theory and practice in his work.

The great physicist J. J. Thompson once stated that research in applied science leads to reforms; research in pure science leads to revolutions. The distinction between pure science and applied science is now, however, quite blurred. Scientists may work on something they consider pure science and then discover later that it has practical applications. Possibly the best example of this is the case of Otto Hahn, who appears to have failed to see the implications of his own work on the atom. His theoretical work was, of course, very instrumental in helping to create the atomic bomb. When the bomb was dropped on Hiroshima Hahn was quite distraught by the idea that he had contributed to this event. Freeman Dyson describes Hahn's grief:

When Otto Hahn stumbled upon the discovery of nuclear fission in Berlin in 1938, he had no inkling of nuclear weapons, no premonition that he was treading on danger-ous ground. When the news of Hiroshima came to him seven years later, he was overcome with such grief that his friends were afraid that he would kill himself.[3]

If a clear distinction between pure science and applied science is no longer tenable, then Thompson's statement takes on a new significance. We are now living in an age when reformation and revolution go together – not just change, but revolutionary change.

As the horizon of science expands, so does the number of its practitioners, the scientists. 'Scientist' is in fact a relatively new word. It was coined by William Whewell when he was President of the British Association in 1841. He used the word to describe a new phenomenon which was just then manifesting itself: the rise of a distinctive group of people who were interested not only in wresting nature's secrets from her, but also in gaining the knowledge to enable them to subdue her capricious ways. This group has become a dominant one in our society. There are many thousands of scientists and more and more money is being poured into scientific endeavours. We are indeed a scientific society.

2. *Science and the Future of Society*

The modern scientific revolution differs, then, from previous ones not only in its scope but also in its very nature. The fusion of knowing and doing has dramatically changed our mastery over ourselves and our environment. There are those who argue, however, that this very mastery is a Pandora's box which, now it is opened, poses a grave threat to humanity. The nature of this threat has been presented most vividly not by the philosophers or theologians but by novelists and film makers. Such novels as E. M. Forster's *The Machine Stops*, Zamyatin's *We*, Aldous Huxley's *Brave New World* and Kurt Vonnegut's *Player Piano*, and films such as Fritz Lang's *Metropolis* and Terry Gilliam's *Brazil*, all conjure up a future society which has been dehumanized by scientific progress. Humans are becoming dehumanized because this 'scientific mentality' conflicts with a true understanding of what it is to be human. Is this a valid assessment of what science is and where it will lead us?

One of the first exponents of science in the modern sense was Galileo who decided to 'leave the world of angels and spirits until he had time for them', and in the meantime rolled little balls down grooves in an inclined plane. Galileo's way of thinking severed theology from science. In the mediaeval period science had been the handmaid of the church, dedicated not so much to the absolute pursuit of truth as to the pursuit of absolute truth. Roger Bacon in the thirteenth century in his *Opus Maius* could claim that the grounds for studying natural science were that it would 'lead the mind through a study of created things to a contemplation of the Creator'. But by the middle of the seventeenth century Galileo's more limited objectives had become the bedrock of the scientific method, and whether there even was a creator had become an irrelevant question for science.[4]

Scientific observation works by isolating effects. When he rolled balls down the inclined plane, Galileo was able to isolate all sorts of irrelevant influences, such as colour or material, and allow for influences such as slope and plane and size of ball. Later Newton was able to use such data in formulating his equations of motion. Unless one concentrates upon only a few effects science of the modern kind is impossible. The success of science, then, depends to a great extent on limiting one's horizon and asking only questions which can be answered by scientific inquiry. This is why it is such folly to extend the scientific method to areas of human endeavour which are, in fact, outside its purview. We have already discussed in our previous chapter the dangers of such application of the scientific method to all fields of human knowledge. Reductionnism of an insidious type is the result, as when, for example, human beings are described as 'nothing but a complex bio-chemical mechanism powered by a combustion system which energizes computers with prodigious storage facilities for the retention of encoded information'.[5] Similarly the description of the human as a 'naked ape' is disconcerting.[6] In reducing humans to machines or animals, we exclude those qualities which make us distinctive. Human beings are animals, of course. And they do have 'prodigious storage facilities' in the brain. But humans are also creative, spontaneous, loving, humorous, artistic. They are, moreover, more than the sum total of all these qualities. There is an essentially mysterious quality about humans which, if overlooked, results in a dehumanized self-image and a bleakly totalitarian society.

Arthur Koestler, in his novel *Arrival and Departure*, describes the thinking in such a totalitarian state. One of the characters (a protagonist for such a state) is speaking:

> Close your eyes. Imagine Europe up to the Urals as an empty space on the map. There are only fields of energy: hydro-power, magnetic ores, coal seams under the earth, oil-wells, forests, vineyards, fertile and barren lands. Connect these sources of energy with blue, red, yellow lines, and you get the distributive network. Draw circles of varying radius around the points of intersection and you get the centre of industrial conglomerations, work out the human labour required to feed the net at any point, and you get the adequate density of population for any district, province or nation; divide this figure by the quantity of horse-power that it produces, and you get the standard of living allotted to it. Wipe out those ridiculous winding boundaries, the Chinese Walls which cut across our fields of energy; scrap or transfer industries which were needlessly built in the wrong places; liquidate the surplus population in areas where they are not required; shift the population of certain districts . . . wipe out . . . the influence of the churches, of overseas capital, of any philosophy or religion, ethical or aesthetic system of the past.[7]

Koestler's book is of course fiction. Nevertheless this quotation illustrates a mode of thinking which is perhaps more prevalent than we care to admit.

Those artists who see the scientific world view as a threat to humanity have a point. Yet what they see as scientific thinking does not square with how most scientists think. Physical sciences do not depend wholly on facts. Science is a way of making sense and pattern out of our experiences, so that it is not the facts themselves, but what we make out of them which is important. And there is no reason why any one pattern should be exhaustive of all meaning and significance. The idea that there is only one way of looking at things is one which most scientists do not hold. In our previous chapter, for example, we noted that different incompatible models may be proposed by scientists to explain the same data, as in the descriptions of the quantum world.

It is essential to realize that there are a number of different models or frameworks which may be used to describe the human situation, and that these determine both the questions that are asked and the answers that are given. Fixation on one kind of question and one kind of answer can only lead to dehumanization. Human experience must be grasped as a totality, and it is quite misguided to accept just one understanding of it, be it scientific or otherwise.

In a scientific society such as ours it is inevitable that there should be large-scale planning. Many important techological developments are impossible without it. The danger in this is that humans come to be seen as merely functional in the technological order of things.[8] This is especially true now that computers have come to govern so much of human life.

Recent developments have indicated that important social and political decisions are now being made on so-called scientific or technical grounds by computers which leave out the 'human factor'. This is more of a problem now than it was when Coulson wrote, but he had enough foresight to see it as a major issue for modernity. Computers are complex machines which can do so many things better than humans. They can learn from experience, and organize data into logical patterns.[9] But it is a mistake to anthropomorphize computers and give them the power of human reason.[10] Unfortunately, because computers are so much more efficient in solving certain types of abstract problems, there is a temptation to think that they are better at making complicated decisions which affect our future. We are thus in danger of handing over our destiny to the computer. In many of his novels Kurt Vonnegut raises the question: In an age in which computerized machines do everything, what are human beings *for*?[11] It is a question which Vonnegut raises with his usual mordant wit, but which is hauntingly insistent in its integrity. Coulson was recognizing this when he said that the key question for human beings today is the one that the psalmist asked centuries ago, 'What is Man?' The question may be put in another way: What is distinctive about humans? It is often said that emotions are distinctively human. But this has become a problematic assertion in an age when certain techniques and drugs are able to create specific emotions in people. What does it say about the authenticity of human emotions when, for example, a religious experience can be engendered by a drug?

In raising questions such as these, Coulson was recognizing that the modern age raises many difficult questions and issues. But his own answer to the question 'What is Man?' was that we are children of God, and this for him was a solid basis on which to approach the problems of the modern age. Moreover, he always balanced the difficulties and disadvantages posed by science and technology against the undoubted benefits which have accrued to humankind as a result of scientific development. It is surely salutary that we no longer have to dig and spin. But we have to be constantly aware of the limits of science and technology. We can see, for example, that the machine is a symbol of rationality and as God is 'Lord of the mind' it can tell us something about God himself. But we must remember that God is also the God of our heart, soul and strength. It is a fatal mistake to reduce human beings to a single dimension. When rationality becomes supreme, it is easy to create a suitable climate for the famous factory notice which read, 'Do not waste the time of this machine.' This is what we have to guard against, and so look the challange of the scientific world directly in the face with neither fear nor facile optimism.

3. *Science, Nationalism and War*

We have stressed the importance of the rise of science in the modern world. Of great significance also is the rise of the nation-state. It is interesting to note that the origins of modern science and of the modern nation-state are almost contemporaneous. In 1648 the Treaty of Westphalia ended the Thirty Years War and marked the beginning of the nation-state. Twelve years later, in 1660, the Royal Society was founded and about the same time the Academies in France and Italy were established. This is generally recognized as the beginning of modern science. For a long time these two developments were quite independent. Inevitably, however, they were driven together by circumstance – the circumstance of modern warfare.

That this link would be forged was not obvious at first. The halting recognition of science as an important element in modern warfare dawned slowly during the First World War. Early in the war, the appointment of a physicist to the consulting board to assist the navy in America was made only because of a chance remark by an assistant to President Wilson to the effect that, 'It might be good to have a mathematician in case we have to calculate something.' The chemists fared no better for when the American Chemical Association offered its assistance to the Secretary of War they were told that it was not necessary because the War Department already had a chemist. By the end of the war, however, the situation had altered radically. Chemical warfare had been introduced and the resources of science were being used to the full. Subsequently it was commonly said that the chemists won the First World War and the physicists the Second.

Science thus became inextricably linked with national goals. Science is power, and the more powerful the nation-state, the more it needs science to keep it that way. In 1946 in the United States the President's Scientific Research Board spoke of science as 'a major factor in national survival'.[12] And what more conclusive evidence of this way of thinking could there be than in the outcry in the United States which followed the launching of Russia's first satellite in 1957? Many Americans perceived this as a direct threat to America's survival as a nation, because it was symbolic of the fact that they had fallen behind in the scientific endeavour. Shortly after his election, President Kennedy poured vast sums of money into the scientific field with the primary object of outstripping the Russians. And now we see where all this is leading, as the 'Star Wars' programme rears its gorgonian head. In this scheme we see clearly silhouetted for us the dark side of the scientific endeavour, as we hand over to computer programmes decisions which will mean life or death for humankind. And it is all done in the name of national security.

There are many who see the link between science and the nation-state as a deadly combination. Coulson was not so pessimistic. He had faith in scientists and felt that as a whole they would act responsibly. He granted that there were some scientists who did not think that the use made of their work was any of their concern. This was a position he found quite untenable, and he did not believe that many scientists held it. There were scientists who refused to work on scientific enterprises which could be used in a destructive way.[13] Most scientists recognize that they are responsible for what they can 'reasonably see' of the 'immediate' use of their findings.[14] In view of the way nations now used science Coulson believed that a responsible scientist had to be politically aware.

Although Coulson had a fundamental faith in scientists, he did not underestimate the difficulties of avoiding the misuse of science. Science (and scientists) were, for example, misused in Nazi Germany. Coulson attributes this in large part to the lack of academic freedom. From 1935 onwards, attendance at scientific congresses in Germany or abroad were subject to approval by the Science Congress centre, an agency of the Reich Ministry of Propaganda. From 1939 onwards, all Ph.D. theses had to be submitted for official Nazi censorship. Coulson thought it essential that scientists should not submit to secrecy. If scientists work in an atmosphere of secrecy, and if they are required to make decisions which cannot be discussed freely and openly, then disastrous consequences may ensue. The case of the eminent physicist Lord Cherwell (a colleague of Coulson's at Oxford) during the Second World War is a good example. It has now emerged that Lord Cherwell advised Churchill to adopt the policy of the obliteration bombing of German cities. Leaving aside the moral question, Lord Cherwell's advice was apparently accepted on scientific grounds, and he was later seen to be in error in his estimates of the damage which would be done. Had other scientists been able to engage in discussion of the consequences, which they were not because of wartime secrecy, the final decision might have been different.

One of the greatest fears people have today is of a nuclear holocaust. It is a great irony that science has increased our mastery over our environment and at the same time put our very survival in jeopardy. As long as people are divided among themselves into nations willing to wage war, nuclear annihilation remains a hideous vista before us, and the link between science and nationalism a darkly problematic one.

4. *The Real Value of Science*

On a brighter note, Coulson believed that science could provide a cohesive force between societies that was strong enough to transcend the narrow concerns of nationalism.[15] Whereas nations may have different political ideologies and criteria for judging artistic endeavours, science remains a common enterprise pursued with common criteria in all nations. So although the world seems to be in a state of disunity, science offers a reasonable prospect for a common enterprise for all nations. Scientists themselves often find their allegiance to the ideals of science transcends national concerns. During the First World War the Royal Society refused to remove German scientists from its list of members, a clear statement that within the scientific community customary frontiers have little significance. Scientists of all persuasions, beliefs and nationalities contribute to scientific inquiry and influence one another.

Not only does science provide a cohesive force within society but by its very nature it is oriented to future possibilities. There is a clash here between science and politics. Politics, at least as conceived in the modern world, is the 'art of the possible' and is pragmatic, focussing upon the present situation. Science is theoretical and predictive, and focusses upon the future. Coulson thought that those with scientific training thus had qualities which enabled them to make a distinctive contribution to political thinking. In this he was anticipating the argument of a recent book, *The Making of the Atomic Bomb* by Richard Rhodes.[16] Rhodes' book is a magisterial effort, noteworthy not only for its extensive treatment of the events leading up to the making of the bomb, but also because it is really an *apologia* for science. It is the most comprehensive and important book of its kind to be published in recent years.[17]

Rhodes goes to great lengths to show that the making of the bomb was not the work of one or even a few men, but was the culmination of the work of the scientific community. This is precisely the same point that Coulson made in his second lecture to the SCM group at Manchester in 1956:

[The development of nuclear energy] needed first Faraday's simple experiments with magnets deflecting an electric current, and J. J. Thompson's imaginative discovery of the deflection of individual electrons and nuclei; Lord Rutherford's scattering experiments to justify the nuclear atom and Madame Curie's radioactivity to show that a nucleus could sometimes split naturally; C. T. R. Wilson's bombarding the atom with other radioactive particles (here alpha-particles), Chadwick's identification of the neutron as one of the most effective of all the 'fundamental particles' in penetration of a nucleus; Hahn's realization a few months before war broke out in 1939 that the heavy atomic nucleus of uranium, when it captured a neutron, would split into two nearly equal parts instead of, as with lighter elements, merely chipping off a small fragment from its surface; it needed all this long cycle of gradually developing knowledge, coupled with Einstein's theory of relativity and the magic equivalent of mass and energy, before an atomic pile could be constructed.[18]

Rhodes' argument that scientists are moral searchers for truth and the 'republic of science' is international in scope and founded on openness is also found in Coulson's writings. But it is in the discussion of science and the modern nation-state that we find the most important parallels between Rhodes and Coulson. Scientists should not be blamed for the nuclear dilemma, says Rhodes, for to do so confuses the message with the messenger. Scientists did not invent nuclear fission, they discovered it. It is the modern nation-state which has used science to protect itself and further its ambitions. But the total annihilation which the bomb is able to bring has so changed political realities that science must eventually destroy the very concept of the nation-state, for the only security from the bomb comes through decreasing national sovereignty:

Rather that a guarantor of sovereignty the arms race has proved a *reductio ad absurdum* of sovereignty. Though they bristle with . . . weapons, the superpowers confront each other today as totally vulnerable, totally dependent for their continued survival on mutual and reasonable restraint, their . . . sovereignties thoroughly compromised . . .[19]

Science fights the exclusivity of the nation-state by sharing its discoveries and encouraging openness. Science transcends national boundaries and sentiments, and confronts the nation-state with 'the facts and probabilities it discovers in the course of its daily work'. Thus:

> Nuclear winter, whatever its level of severity, is one of those probabilities. Damage to the ozone layer is another. The likelihood of widespread epidemics after a nuclear war and of mass starvation because of disruption of food transport are two more. Each new contribution to understanding – more knowledge turned over to mankind – must further erode that stubborn and genocidal ignorance [of the nation-state].[20]

The similarity to Coulson's line of argument is striking. The positive value of science is that it is a common enterprise founded on openness and trust and which is future-oriented. These are sentiments which Rhodes and Coulson share. But there is one significant difference between them. While Coulson thinks that science may indeed help to provide a cohesive force in society, he does not think that by itself it is enough. Rhodes, on the other hand, has elevated science to a status similar to that of a revelatory religion. In his scheme of things, if anything can save us, science will by revealing the true state of affairs. But science is an abstraction. It has no independent life of its own, and by itself can do nothing. It is people who do science and who ultimately bear the burden of responsibility for its use and misuse. This was something that Coulson understood very well, and as a scientist himself was well qualified to speak about. It is to the question of responsibility in a scientific age that we now turn.

Chapter Five

Responsibility in a Scientific Age

1. *The Scientific Task*

We have seen that Coulson emphasized the importance of understanding how the accelerating growth of science would have turbulent effects upon society. The effects of science thus become a political matter, and as a result scientists find themselves (often reluctantly) in the political arena. As science provides power, it is inevitably pressed into the service of governments, and scientists become faced with complex political questions about their work. Should they ignore the use governments may make of their work? If not, what are the best ways to control the uses made of what they do? What, in short, is the exact nature of the scientist's responsibility to society?

When faced with these complex questions, those speaking on behalf of science (and they are not necessarily all professional scientists) often claim either too much or too little. In our previous chapter we saw how they claim too much when they claim that science itself can provide the answers to all the problems which arise from it. Science provides understanding of how the world works. It cannot go beyond that to answer the question of whether things ought to be other than what they are. But if it is wrong to claim too much on behalf of science, it is equally wrong to claim too little, as in the argument that science is an ethically neutral endeavour which may be legitimately divorced from its practical consequences. It is true of course that scientists cannot be expected to foresee all the possible uses to which their work may be put. Coulson often quoted the eminent physician Percy Bridgeman as saying that if he were to take personal responsibility for ensuring that all of his discoveries were put to beneficial use, he would spend almost all of his time seeking the advice of some kind of forecasting bureau and then lobbying the government to procure the necessary legislation. So there is obviously a limit to the responsibility of the scientist and he cannot be held responsible for every possible use made of his work. After all, a hammer may be used to drive nails into wood or to crack someone's skull!

To say, however, that a scientist cannot be held accountable for all the possible uses of his work is not to say that science itself is neutral. Scientists themselves often have premonitions of the significance of their work. During the latter stages of the First World War Rutherford wrote to a friend saying that he thought his experiment on the breaking of the nucleus of the atom would eventually turn out to be more important than the war which was just ending. At the time it must have seemed an extremely extravagant claim, but Rutherford was, of course, right. And once it became possible to envisage harnessing the power of the atom, it became obvious that such power would be used by governments, and nuclear power would become a political issue. Indeed, the development of so many scientific organizations formed especially to deal with the social implications and responsibilities of scientists (e.g. the Society for Social Responsibility in Science) indicates that the majority of scientists themselves do not believe that science is ethically neutral. Coulson certainly did not think so.[1]

While he did not subscribe to the view that science was ethically neutral, neither did Coulson think that science was to be regarded with suspicion and controlled. Time and again he spoke out against imposing arbitrary controls on science. In his fourth Pegram lecture he spoke intensely about the threat posed to science by those who wished to restrict its activities. In 1927 the Bishop of Ripon had suggested that 'the sum of human happiness outside scientific circles would not necessarily be reduced if for ten years every physical and chemical laboratory were closed and the patient and resourceful energy in them transferred to recovering the lost art of getting on together and finding the formula for making both ends meet in the scale of human life'. It was a statement which greatly offended Coulson. It was offensive because it failed to understand the important, positive role science had to play in the world. It is, moreover, 'blasphemous' to attempt to restrict freedom of thought. These two points – first, that science has an important task to perform, and second, that freedom of scientific (indeed all) thought is sacrosanct, are constant themes throughout Coulson's writings and lectures. We must now expand upon what he says about them.

One of the tasks of science was a very practical one: to help remove what Coulson called the 'evil spectres' of hunger and poverty. As chairman of Oxfam he had many opportunities to visit impoverished parts of the world, and he was very struck by how daunting the task of eliminating these evils was. Although we can isolate other individual problems as well as poverty and hunger – such as disease, illiteracy and overpopulation – they are in reality all part of one larger problem, that of underdevelopment. Many countries are simply not equipped to deal with the increasing demands made on their resources in order adequately to feed, clothe and shelter their people. Science can help with this endeavour by helping to develop resources in a responsible way. In particular, practical help was needed, not vague advice or exhortation:

> Now it is no good telling people who are grossly undernourished and illiterate that they must not have children. For some of them this represents one of the very few ways in which they can express their natural human relationships. We must do something more realistic than merely give advice.[2]

Gandhi had said, 'To the millions of people who do not have anything like two meals a day, the only decent form in which God dare appear would be food.' It was a sentiment often echoed by Coulson, who believed that all people with a sense of responsibility are called to a great creative task in the sharing of wealth: 'If we really believe that we are members of one family, then we ought surely to be deeply dissatisfied that so little is done to help.'[3]

Coulson outlined some of the areas in which help was desperately needed in his little book, *Science, Technology and the Christian*. First, underdeveloped countries need to develop their own sources of energy. There is no doubt that the passage of time since Coulson wrote has proved him quite right on this score. We are very much aware these days of the importance of energy, especially in formulating national economic strategies. Coulson thought, however, that the great contribution scientists could make here was through developing nuclear power.

> We can therefore see that nothing less than an almost complete nuclear power supply will be suitable for a large part of the world. Without it, not only would our own civilization slowly grind to a halt, but there would be no foreseeable development in the underdeveloped countries of the world.[4]

The second great contribution science can make is in providing the knowledge which will enable underdeveloped countries to produce more food. To illustrate how urgent this need was, Coulson several times repeated the poignant story of the man who was so weak from hunger that he did not have enough strength to eat the food a nun had brought to him. His dying words were: 'You should have come yesterday.' For the long term Coulson always supported the idea that aid societies should, by providing scientific advice and professional expertise, seek to help underdeveloped countries produce their own food. Charity, over the long term, is not enough. This becomes quite clear in his address on 'Commitment' delivered to an Oxfam youth discussion in 1966:

> For many young people one way of doing something is personally to go, under VSO or IVS or some other auspices, and enter into the life and suffering of the people whom we wish to serve. For my own part I hope that before I die I shall have been able to do a spell of some sort of service in one of the developing countries. This short-term aid does two things. On the one hand it provides help just when and where it is most needed; and on the other hand it

carries with it that sense of human solidarity and human compassion that is often just as important as the merely physical aid.[5]

Helping feed the hungry is not simply a matter of sending food parcels, it is more effectively done by rendering practical assistance.

The problem of hunger is intricately bound up with the problem of overpopulation. The population of the world has grown dramaticaly and continues to grow at the rate of 158 per minute. *The Guinness Book of Records* gives the past and present world population as follows:

Date	Millions
8000 BC	*c.* 6
AD 1	*c.* 255
1000	*c.* 254
1250	416
1500	460
1600	579
1700	679
1800	954
1900	1633
1920	1862
1930	2070
1940	2295
1950	2513
1960	3049
1970	3678
1975	4033
1980	4415
1985	4837
1987	5000[6]

Notice the increasing differences in the population figures compared with the shortening spans between the years. The more the population increases, the greater the challenge to produce more food. We cannot all live off the land any more, but must rely on improved scientific techniques to produce more food from smaller areas. If the population were not to increase then (at least theoretically) there would be more food to go around. Although Coulson did not countenance simply telling hungry people to stop having so many children, he did strongly advocate birth control.[7]

We have said that at least 'in theory' if the world population were to stabilize or go down there would be less hunger. In fact we know that simply controlling the world population would not alleviate hunger. Producing food and distributing it are two different matters. Effective distribution depends upon social and political factors. We have become all too familiar with food distribution being severely hindered by internecine political strife (as in Ethiopia) or bureaucratic corruption (as on the Indian subcontinent). Such instances have led many people to despair of ever feeding the hungry where there has not been social and political reform. Calls for such changes add another cloudy dimension to the issues, as many individuals (and sometimes governments) refuse to help countries they suspect of being 'left-wing'. The humanitarian question of how the hungry of the world should be fed thus becomes embroiled in ideological argument. It is noteworthy that Coulson, who took stances on some issues which suggested 'left-wing' leanings,[8] refrained from giving political prescriptions to cure the world's ills. He never thought adherence to ideologies such as socialism or capitalism could in themselves bring about the Kingdom of God on earth. Certainly it was not the job or the desire of scientists to seek change through such ideological means. As he put it: 'Scientists want a scientific community, not a scientific party.' In *Science, Technology and the Christian* Coulson discusses the international character of science and technology and concludes that by themselves they are not enough to provide a wide-scale, dominant and cohesive belief for the Western world.[9] Nevertheless, he did believe that a simple prerequisite of justice was a democratic and corruption-free government:

[If] we are prepared to make the necessary changes in administration, in land tenure, in local custom, and in economic production and distribution, the job [of feeding the hungry nations] could be done.[10]

Coulson believed, then, that co-operation with scientists could help alleviate, if not eliminate, the evils of poverty and hunger. Thus the Bishop of Ripon in his call for a moratorium on scientific research had failed to understand how essential science was to survival in the modern world. But more than that, the bishop's suggestion would strike at the very heart of science by seeking to limit free and unfettered inquiry. We have already seen how Coulson abhorred the very idea of limiting scientific inquiry. He strongly endorsed the view of the Society for Freedom in Science which held that science has a value which is independent of the practical benefits it yields to society. If the freedom of science is restricted, it cannot serve the practical and the cultural needs of society. But even more, to deny freedom in scientific inquiry is to deny the principle of freedom of thought.

One of the reasons Coulson spent so much of his time addressing public gatherings is that he thought he had a responsibility, as a scientist, to inform and educate the public about what he and other scientists were doing and thinking. Thus in the prologue to his *Science, Technology and the Christian* he says:

> The only excuse for writing this book is that I believe it to be exceedingly important in any democracy that ordinary people should know enough about the factors which affect and influence their lives as will enable them to recognize the problems which have to be solved.[11]

The suspicion with which much of the public regards scientists will only be overcome by educating and informing the public. These tasks therefore become an important part of scientific responsibility. This is especially important in an age when scientists can not only create weapons of mass destruction, but can also change almost all the aspects of our ordinary life.

The alchemists of the Middle Ages believed that public knowledge of science's secrets would lead to the abuse of its power. In a way both the hopes and the fears of the alchemists have been realized in the modern age. In their quest to turn base metals into gold, the alchemists were trying to uncover the essential secret of the transmutation of essences. Nuclear physicists have now achieved this, and enormous power has been put at the disposal of many who are perhaps unfit to wield it. But Coulson does not share the pessimism of the alchemists. He vigorously defends scientists who, he claims, are a very responsible group. 'It is my own experience that among all the different groups of people with whom I have been involved, the scientific group, *as a whole*, is the one most aware of this responsibility.'[12] His writings abound with references to scientists who showed restraint and responsibility in their work.

> Leonardo da Vinci invented a submarine, but because he felt that such knowledge would be used for evil purposes, he did not make it known. Robert Boyle . . . invented some poisons, and a form of invisible ink, which he refused to divulge. The Italian Tartaglia devised a new and better form of gunnery, but declined to make it known to the armies and the generals, because they would use such knowledge for evil purposes . . .[13]

Despite Coulson's defence of scientists, however, he was not a naïve optimist. He recognized that we faced an uncertain scientific future, which could easily go wrong.

2. Responsibility, Science, and the Human Prospect

In his recent book, *The Imperative of Responsibility*, Hans Jonas says:

> What we must avoid at all cost is determined by what we must preserve at all cost, and this in turn is predicated on the 'image of man' we entertain. Formerly, this image was enshrined in the teachings of revealed religions. With their eclipse today, secular reason must base the normative concept of man on a cogent, at least persuasive, doctrine of general being: metaphysics must underpin ethics.[14]

> Faith in revealed truth can very well supply the foundation for ethics, but it is not there on command, and not even the strongest argument of need permits resorting to a faith that is absent or discredited.[15]

Jonas is a true representative of much contemporary thinking about responsibility. He believes that the appeal to revelation no longer carries conviction in the modern world, and that therefore it is imperative to argue for responsibility on some other ground. Jonas' own effort is a highly learned attempt to ground the notion of responsibility in metaphysics. Coulson, on the other hand, as a convinced Christian, never considered revealed religion to be discredited and therefore quite candidly appealed to it when speaking of the need for responsibility. It is an open question whether Jonas' philosophically abstruse reasoning is ultimately more convincing than Coulson's unabashed appeal to revelation.

It is not surprising that Coulson should ground his appeal for scientific responsibility in Christian faith. We have already seen how he argued that not only were Christianity and science quite compatible but they in fact shared intimately similar features. He believed that studying science was a religious activity through which we could gain some insight into the mind of God. And this is why he could speak of being 'thrilled' by science:

> These are thrilling events [in science]. But they are by no means unique, and are typical of the new age into which we are now passing. There is something very fine about the temper of the scientists of today, which has 'spilled over' to the larger industrialists, giving them the confidence and faith that match the scale on which they must think . . . [Their] vision, courage and calculated faith not only redound to the credit of the human mind, but also reflect in a measure something of the mind of God Himself. J. B. Conant . . . spoke of the ideas and practices of modern science as if they were a monument, 'fit to be compared with the Parthenon of Ancient Greece and the great Gothic Cathedrals of the Middle Ages', as a witness to what the flowering of the human spirit can achieve.[16]

Coulson would certainly, however, have agreed with Jonas that the 'image of man' which we entertain is determinative of the way we think about responsibility. In his address to the Oxfam Youth Group in 1966 he made the point that how countries develop depends as much on their view of humanity as it does on their technologists and scientists.[17] And in *Some Problems of the Atomic Age* he says:

> Our decisions, at every level, do ultimately depend on what we think about the nature of God and, as a consequence, upon the nature and status of man.[18]

> [There is within us] the still small voice, compelling, insistent, reminding us that the important thing, the place where you begin, is not the state, nor the power of the atom, nor the mighty machines of industry, it is the heart of man, held within the hand of God.[19]

And in *Responsibility*:

> Any significant thinking about responsibility is ultimately thinking about what makes us really human, and its right exercise the best indication of our humanity.[20]

Responsibility for Christians means recognizing that we are made in the image of God, and that what we do should reflect that.[21] Since science is fundamentally a religious activity through which we discern something of the mind of God, it is important that Christians do not shirk the responsibility of correctly using science by simply dismissing it as somehow nefarious. In his *Ryecroft Papers* George Gissing said:

> I hate and fear science because of my conviction that, for a long time to come, if not forever, it will be the remorseless enemy of mankind. I see it destroying all simplicity and gentleness of life, all the beauty of the world, I see it darkening men's minds and hardening their hearts.[22]

And Otto van der Sprenkel had sardonically remarked, 'Vacuum cleaners corrupt, washing machines corrupt absolutely.' Coulson regarded such views as quite wrong. 'Once again the Christian has his duty – it is the obligation to assert that despite all misconceptions and all fear, science is a work of God.'[23]

As humans are children of God, they have the responsibilities as well as the privileges which go with that status. Without this conviction that the human race is the family of God, science will be misused and a darkness will fall on our future. Schrödinger, the famous polymath, had said that it was impossible to explain in purely logical terms the 'shall' of Kant's categorical imperative. Coulson agreed with him. He went further, however, and said that one may only move from an 'is' to an 'ought' through an act of religious faith. Science by its very nature can only describe how things are, not how they ought to be. There are those who have tried to argue moral postulates from supposed scientific premises, as in the case of those who have argued for a 'Darwinian morality'. Darwinism teaches us (so the argument goes) that only the fittest survive. This is nature's way of telling us what is good. The good is that which survives. Thus Herbert Spencer could argue that only conduct which promotes the survival of the human race is good, and if this means that the weak have to die, then so be it. But this view, although appearing since Spencer in various modified forms, has been abandoned by most thinking people, as Thomas Huxley (a former friend of Spencer's) publicly acknowledged as long ago as 1893.

Coulson's best example to show how science had to be grounded in a religious imperative concerned the medical profession. The Hippocratic Oath, dating from the fifth century BC and reaffirmed at a World Medical Conference in 1948, states a laudable principle – that doctors should always serve the best interests of humanity. But the application of the principle to practice has always proved problematic. Those doctors in Hitler's concentration camps who experimented on human beings often justified themselves by claiming that the medical knowledge they obtained in this way was invaluable. Their work benefited the many at the expense of a few. We recoil from such an argument, yet there is a grotesque logic in it. It is hard to see how one could condemn it on purely scientific grounds. It is quite clear to Coulson that science alone cannot provide suitable moral guidelines in such questions: responsibility loses its moorings if it is not tied to religious faith.

Coulson recognized, of course, that those who shared his convictions were a minority. But this was not a reason to despair, rather it called for even greater responsibility on the part of this minority, for a creative minority can decisively influence the majority. The word responsibility comes from the verb 'to respond', that is, 'to make a movement towards someone, to react, and in that movement to express human solidarity'.[24] F. H. Heinemann thought that the virtue of responsibility could be summed up in the phrase (deliberately echoing Descartes) '*Respondeo, ergo sum*' – 'I respond, therefore I am.' But Coulson thought that the essence of responsibility was better captured in the phrase '*Respondeo, etsi mutabor*' – 'I respond, even though I shall be changed.'[25] Responsibility implies change. It implies thinking through what we have become and what we are to become. We are called to think creatively about this change.

In response to this challenge Coulson did not restrict his comments merely to stating general principles. He was quite prepared to discuss specific practical issues and suggest what a responsible course of action would be. An instructive way of summarizing Coulson's views on responsibility would be to examine what he said about a couple of these issues, namely ecology and economics.

Coulson did not use the term ecology, which gained vogue only later, but if he did not use the term, he certainly addressed the issue. He often referred to the non-human world as the 'world of things'. As we have already seen, Coulson thought that the world of things was important to God in its own right. The creation story in Genesis emphasizes this. If 'things' are important to God, they should be important to us. Coulson therefore came out strongly against despoilation of the countryside, increasing the urban sprawl, and pollution of the environment by atomic radiation. He was particularly emphatic in his opposition to the atmospheric nuclear tests of the 1950s, calling them a 'sacrilege'.[26] It is very doubtful whether he would have thought any better of the underground tests of the 1970s and 1980s, especially now that it has become known that radiation from them has often leaked into the atmosphere. Coulson's stand on these environmental issues is certainly relevant to today's situation. Undoubtedly, had he lived he would have found that he had much in common with the 'green' movements.

It has already been noted how, in the area of economics, Coulson thought that it was imperative that the Western world should aid the developing countries not only with sums of money, but also by giving practical help. He called, moreover, for a global view of the use of resources which took into account the needs of all peoples of all nations. The same principles which governed his views on global economic problems also informed his views on domestic issues. He openly criticized the idea that profit should be the criterion for deciding national economic strategies. If we cannot abolish the profit motive, then at the very least we should seek ways to 'control' or 'sublimate' it. He also criticized the commitment to unlimited economic growth. We should be building a society which can function cohesively within an 'economic stationary equilibrium'. Finally, as a society we must think through carefully the consequences of the 'labour revolution' in which so many people cannot find work.

There seems little doubt that Coulson would have found himself repeating these same points were he alive today. He had been disturbed by the political slogans of the 1959 election which appealed solely to human self-interest.[27] He would surely have been appalled to see how political strategies in Britain today were dictated by a market economics which by its very nature is unable to take account of distinctively human considerations.

These examples of what Coulson had to say about ecology and economic issues illustrate how the principles which guided him in dealing with them are as relevant today as they were when he was speaking. In the modern world thinking through what responsibility means is an immensely difficult task. Coulson recognised this, but believed that we can be successfully guided in that task by a creative spirit, a Christian sense of humanity, and a clear-headed common sense.[28] We are still in charge of our own destiny. There is a Talmudic parable about a rabbi who had a reputation for being able to read people's thoughts. One day a mischievous boy decided to put him to the test. He took a living bird in his hand and went to the rabbi and said, 'Rabbi, I have a bird in my hand behind my back. Tell me, is it alive or dead?' The boy thought to himself, if he says it is alive I shall squeeze it to death and then open my hand and show it to him, and if he says it is dead, I shall open my hand and it will fly away. The rabbi, however, merely replied, 'As you will, as you will.' This is how Coulson sees the future. It will be what we make it. There is a French saying about bureaucrats, 'They know everything and nothing else.' It was Coulson's hope that this would not be the verdict of the future on that creative minority[29] which bears the burden of responsibility for future developments in science and technology.

Having discussed Coulson's views on scientific responsibility, it is time to turn to a discussion of just how significant these views are in the contemporary context. Our next chapter accordingly seeks to draw out further the implications of Coulson's views on intellectual and social responsibility.

Chapter Six

Coulson in the Contemporary Context

1. *The Need for Intellectual Responsibility*

In an article in *The Guardian* (2 May 1988), Hugh Montefiore lamented the decline of Christianity in Britain today. He concluded his discussion of the reasons for such a decline by saying that Christianity had 'lost the intellectual high ground'. He went on: 'People think that the natural and social sciences have, if not disproved Christianity, at least raised some unanswerable questions, and the same with historical studies. Poets, artists and novelists look elsewhere for inspiration. Until this intellectual high ground is regained, faith cannot prosper.' He then adds pointedly, 'Christianity must be more concerned with truth.'

These sentiments reiterate perfectly those which Coulson expressed over thirty years ago. If there was one overwhelming concern which guided his non-scientific writings, it was the desire to give Christianity intellectual integrity. During his undergraduate days in Cambridge, after being 'spiritually renewed', Coulson wrote a letter to a friend in which he said, 'I have thought it over, and when the emotion has subsided I believe I am able to give perfectly satisfactory reasons for my belief.'[1] This conviction never left him, and is one of the keys to understanding why he devoted so much time to writing about science and religion, for during this period there were not many people who thought that science and religion could be intellectually reconciled.[2] As we have seen, Coulson himself argued that the conflict between science and religion was a modern phenomenon. But he also acknowledged that Christianity had at least in part brought this on itself by so injudiciously attacking many scientific developments. Thus it became necessary for him and others to try to heal the breach which had opened up between science and religion. As both a scientist and a Christian Coulson was ideally suited to understand both worlds, and as someone who was a scientific authority and deeply devout his views carried weight in both camps. But he did not misuse his stature, and always wanted his ideas to be judged on their own merits. The need for intellectual integrity extended to his own ideas as well as those of Christianity. We would do him a disservice if we did not examine his views critically and dispassionately.

Coulson's commitment to a religion of the intellect as well as of the emotions has to be recognized as of great significance in the modern context. Montefiore is right: Christianity can never flourish if it is not intellectually responsible. This means not only being committed to truth, but being open to discussion and change. There is strong resistance among some Christians to such a commitment, revealing a subliminal fear of inquiring too deeply into the espoused truths of Christianity. There is also a persistent belief that religion is really about feeling, that it is directed to the emotions and not to the intellect. Now it is true that many Christians, especially Protestants, have tended to internalize and privatize Christian belief. But this should not overshadow the fact that there has been a strong intellectual tradition in Christianity. Coulson is an heir of this tradition. He himself was a Methodist, and Methodists in particular have been singled out as holding a religion of the heart and not of the head. Don Cupitt, for example, claims that Methodism 'internalized belief' and 'moved away from cosmology' and from 'finding God in the world of nature to finding him at work in the human soul'.[3] It is fortunate for us that Coulson knew his Methodism better than Cupitt and did not 'move away from cosmology'! For Wesley himself had said, 'Properly speaking, we have no Idea of God. We come to our knowledge of his very existence, not from any idea of him, but from our reasoning upon the works of the visible creation.'[4] The *Wesley Naturalist* said about Wesley that he 'claimed and magnified the dignity and greatness of the intellect . . . and eagerly studied, and ultimately taught, the newly realized and expanding science, and interpretations of nature, of his age'.[5] Coulson was being quite true to Christianity in general and his own tradition in particular when he insisted that Christianity should have intellectual responsibility. The Christian must, moreover, use his intellect to find God in the external world, and not rest content with a God who is found only in the soul. A privatized, internalized religion soon degenerates into a religion of mere feeling and preference, without substance or relevance. Coulson realized this and has given a clear lead for others to follow.

If it is to be intellectually responsible then Christianity must be prepared to engage in discussion of the key issues of the day. No issue is more pressing today than science and its effects on society, and Coulson rightly insisted that its relationship to Christianity must be thoroughly and honestly examined. He himself argued that science was a religious activity, and science and religion shared fundamental and common features. It is a constructive avenue of approach to the dialogue between science and religion, as long as it is clearly understood that it is an argument by analogy. Coulson was sometimes misunderstood here. He was not arguing for a common epistemological basis for science and religion, but that similarities between the universes of discourse of science and religion suggests an elusive and multifaceted reality not completely grasped by any one description of it. In formulating this argument Coulson showed the shortcomings of reductionism, an important contribution in its own right.

Human beings have not been around very long when we consider the age of the universe. For Coulson this meant that the world of things is important to God in and of itself: God delights in the world for its own sake. There is a natural resistance (springing from hubris?) to the idea that the world might have a value to God independent of its human occupation. Even when this idea finds expression it is not easily accepted. For example, over two centuries ago, John Balguy wrote that God might have 'various ends and designs of which we have no conception'. But he was vigorously attacked by Thomas Beyes who replied by saying that this was a 'melancholy conclusion, implying that God might have ends other than the happiness of his creatures in creating the universe'. Beyes went on at length to 'prove' that God's only purpose was the happiness of his creatures.[6] He could not conceive of an integral link between God's purposes and the world itself. But Coulson could. In 1973 in a sermon at Cambridge on 'God and things' Coulson noted that Ps. 24.1 says, 'The world *and* they that dwell therein' and concluded that the 'significance of this vast universe is not reducible to human concerns'. In another context when speaking of God and things[7] Coulson noted that it was Ian Fraser who had said, 'We have been interested in nature only insofar as it helped man.' This, says Coulson, represents 'an emasculated doctrine of creation'. In the creation story God spends five days creating 'things' before he turns to creating humankind. When he walked in the Garden, it was not to spy out the nakedness of Adam and Eve, but because 'it [the whole of creation] was very good'. We should not, says Coulson, be afraid to rejoice in the things of this world, as they themselves reflect the joy of creation.[8] That the world might have its own significance for God should not be a 'melancholy conclusion'!

The incarnation focusses our attention on the 'embodied' nature of humankind. We are psychosomatic beings – not, as the ancient Greeks taught, disembodied souls merely inhabiting a body. More and more it is being realized that this has all kinds of implications for our behaviour in the world. If the world is not a strange and foreign place, which we are merely 'passing through', but is in a very real sense part and parcel of God's plan, then it behoves us to treat it with reverence and respect. The world is not there merely so that we can manipulate and exploit it. Manipulative science and exploitation of the world's resources without regard for consequences is wrong.

There is no doubt that had his life not been cut short Coulson would have expanded on these ideas. As it is he has left us enough to know what his thoughts were. These are given in a nutshell in a review of *Honest to God*, in which he asserts that the creation story shows the importance of earthly

things. There is a 'sacramental quality' about the material
universe. God enjoyed the physical world, and in order that
we may enjoy it he gave us a *magisterium* over it.[9] Such a
magisterium implies a responsibility towards the world. Coulson then links this concern for 'down-to-earthness' with the
need to help the underdeveloped countries. His view of the
'world of things' thus forms the link between what he says
about the need for intellectual responsibility and his thinking
on social responsibility.

2. *The Need for Social Responsibility*

Coulson's insistence on social responsibility is at odds with the
pietistic understanding of religion. There have always been
Christians who have stressed pietism, an atittude which
emphasizes individual spirituality and encourages passivity
towards worldly affairs. And in Methodism the doctrine of
perfectionism has encouraged some to direct their attention
inwards on the soul rather than outwards on the concerns of
fellow humans. But once again too much should not be made
of this. In an address to the Tenth World Methodist Conference Coulson said:

> The perfection which is Christ can only be seen when it is
> expressed. So Christian perfection has an immediate ethical
> consequence . . . It is in relationship to our fellows that the
> spirit of perfection is clothed in flesh and blood. So St
> Augustine in his *Civitas Dei*: 'How could the city of God
> take a beginning or be developed, or attain to its proper
> destiny if the life of the saints were not a social life?' . . .
> Our doctrine of perfection is relevant because it asserts that
> all this tumultuous world can be redeemed, and in all the
> patterns of change and revolution, questions of the 'spirit'
> cannot be separated from questions of the 'body'.[10]

In short, Christian perfectionism implies social responsibility.
   There is no doubt that his involvement with the Cambridge
Methodist Group Movement during his undergraduate years
exercised a formative influence on Coulson's own attitude
towards social responsibility. Marcus Ward, who participated
in the Group, once recalled that 'the real genius of the Group is

the insistence on "no expression without impression" and vice versa . . .'[11] And in a memo from the Cambridge Group entitled 'The Oxford and Cambridge Groups: A Summary Survey'[12] the Oxford Group is criticized for having no developed sense of social activity: 'They have little or no social gospel.' But if the Group initially gave Coulson his sense of social responsibility he was well able – as we have seen – to integrate it into his intellectual scheme of things.[13] His concern for social responsibility was not, in other words, some kind of emotional hangover from his Cambridge days; it was, so to speak, part of the intellectual scaffolding which he erected around his faith.

As he was a scientist it is natural that Coulson's concern for social responsibility should manifest itself especially in thinking about scientific responsibility. Since, as Oppenheimer put it, 'the bomb blew to pieces the idea of disinterested science' there have been many who have been deeply suspicious of scientists and the scientific enterprise. Coulson, however, always defended both science and its practitioners, for although science may not be 'value-free' it is not evil. Indeed, science is a gift of God: 'God meant us to possess our modern knowledge.'[14] God means us to 'develop, learn, create'.[15] There can therefore be no retreat from the scientific enterprise. Yet it has to be recognized that there is an ambiguous nature to scientific development; not all of its developments are beneficial. The best example of this ambiguous characteristic is, of course, the splitting of the atom. This has led to the atomic bomb and the nuclear power station. So the responsible use of science becomes problematic. How are we to be guided in our use of science? This is the problem to which Coulson addressed himself in his later years and in one of his writings, *The Scientist's Responsibility in Society*, he espoused an important principle: scientists should only be held responsible for what they can reasonably foresee. In other words, someone like Otto Hahn, who as we mentioned in chapter 4 was extremely distraught to think that his work had contributed to the making of the atomic bomb, should not be seen as culpable. Hahn could not reasonably foresee the use to which his work might have been put. This is an important statement, as there are those in the contemporary debate who suggest that unless we can clearly foresee the direction of a scientific development, we should not proceed with it.[16] For Coulson, of course, it is a question of scientific and academic freedom. To impose arbitrarily restrictions on science was anathema to him. But this does not imply that scientists themselves should not voluntarily relinquish certain scientific endeavours. This is what Coulson himself did when he refused to collaborate on further development of the atomic bomb after the war. And he often commended those scientists who had voluntarily refused to reveal knowledge which might be used for destructive purposes. Thus for Coulson the responsibility of the scientist is entirely an individual matter. It is the scientists themselves who must make the decisions about their work. But – and this is important – scientists have to recognize that science itself will not provide the guidelines on how science should be used. Coulson often echoed the words of B. H. Streeter, 'Science is not enough.'[17] And although a scientist must make an individual decision, no scientist operates in isolation. Scientists are part of a scientific community. It is this community which sustains their work. But their sense of responsibility must be informed by a wider community than the scientific one. Here again we see the link between Coulson's earlier non-scientific writings on science and religion and his later ones on responsibility. There is a kind of 'hidden agenda' in his early writings on science and religion. He is seeking to make scientists feel 'spiritually at home' within the Christian tradition. In turn Christians should encourage and appreciate the efforts of scientists to be faithful to their (God-given) calling, especially with regard to their efforts in the areas of development, peace and education. Coulson believed that if we encouraged scientists to make an 'act of reflection' they would come to realize that only in the Christian tradition could they find adequate resources to deal with the burden of responsibility placed upon them by scientific development.

There is an excellent example to illustrate how science itself does not have the resources to deal adequately with modern scientific problems. It concerns the issue of genetic engineering to which we alluded in chapter 2. In an article in *Cosmopolitan* William Murray when discussing genetic engineering says:

> Dr Haldane (the late British geneticist) predicted that we might breed, for one thing, a race of legless mutants with prehensile tails or feet for space travel. Other scientists would like to see . . . human beings with gills to facilitate underwater travel, people with two kinds of hands, one for heavy work, the other for lighter tasks . . .[18]

Now it would be easy to dismiss this as bizarre nonsense. But it would also be a mistake. The importance of this article lies not in its details, but in the attitude of mind it betrays. Genetic engineering is placed in the context of the general quest to enhance specific human functions. In other words, it is about what humans can or may be able to do, not about what they are. If we consider humans to be no more than a collection of molecules, then it really does not matter how that collection is assembled. Carl Sagan, for example, has said, 'I am a collection of water, calcium and organic molecules called Carl Sagan . . . Some people find this idea somehow demeaning to human dignity. For myself, I find it elevating.'[19] According to this, Carl Sagan would be Carl Sagan even if he were a legless mutant specifically bred for space travel. But are humans to be understood solely in these functional terms? This is a question which it is well to ask not only in the context of genetic engineering,[20] but also in the wider context of all scientific development. Coulson tells this delightful but familiar anecdote to make the point:

> F. A. Cockin, Bishop of Bristol, tells how one day he was sitting in a London tram when a very immaculate gentleman entered, resplendent in his pin-stripe trousers, bowler hat and tightly rolled umbrella. A small boy, sitting opposite, eyed him most suspiciously for a minute or two and then, in that high pitched querulous tone of voice which small boys reserve for really important occasions, he turned to his mother and said: 'Mummy, what's that man *for*?' He was right. There are questions about man which do not

come into the normal cetegories of science – perfectly valid questions, which do not allow those people who having once perceived them to rest until some satisfying answer has been given.[21]

If the only answer we can give to the question 'What are we for?' is a functional one, then there is no telling where developments such as genetic engineering may lead us.

The question 'What is Man?' was one which came to dominate Coulson's thoughts more and more in his later years. He dealt with it explicitly in a lecture in Australia in 1969,[22] in which we see clearly how his view of what it means to be human is grounded in religious suppositions. In it he gives two 'clues' to what it means to be human. First, this is God's world and we are part of God's plan. Second, we are children of God. This means that simple empirical descriptions do not exhaust what we are, because humans have to be placed in a teleological context: they have a purpose, God's purpose.

For those who, like Hans Jonas, regard religious beliefs as 'discredited',[23] an ethic like Coulson's which is based explicitly on religious faith will appear irrelevant. Jonas, as we have seen, does not think that Christianity has the resources to provide an ethic of responsibility for the technological society. He certainly agrees, however, that there is a need for an ethic of responsibility, otherwise we are doomed to certain ecological or nuclear disaster. He thus wrestles with his own question: 'How can enthusiasm for Utopia be transformed into enthusiasm for austerity?' Put in simpler terms, he is wondering how we can make people realize the need for responsibility when it may involve some sacrifice on their part. He is to be commended for attempting to give philosophical reasons for adopting such austerity, but it is doubtful whether he in the end succeeds.[24] A Christian might be tempted to point out that it is no coincidence that the two great philosophies of modern times – those of Nietzsche and Heidegger – have no ethic of social responsibility.[25] Modern philosophy has yet to prove that it has more resources than Christianity when it comes to providing a social ethic for our times. For Coulson it definitely had not.[26]

3 . A Final Question

We have noted already that Coulson stands firmly in the tradition of Wesley when speaking of his commitment to intellectual responsibility. This is also evident in his thought on social responsibility. Coulson rejects quite firmly the 'dualist' position usually associated with Lutheranism. Luther maintained that a Christian should acknowledge the value of this world, but keep the life of faith distinct from it:

> There are two kingdoms, one the kingdom of God, the other the kingdom of this world . . . God's kingdom is a kingdom of grace and mercy . . . but the kingdom of the world is a kingdom of wrath and severity . . . Now he who would confuse these two . . . would put wrath into God's kingdom and mercy into the world's kingdom, and that is the same as putting the devil in heaven and God in hell. [27]

In contrast to the Lutheran position Coulson stresses Christian involvement in and for the world. The incarnation shows God cared for the world, and science, being of singular importance in the world, cannot be divorced from Christian faith. As we have seen in chapter 3, Coulson argues that science is a religious activity, and as such Christians must work through it to produce a better world. Whereas Luther's position may be called dualist, Coulson's position may be called conversionist. It is basically a Wesleyan position. It is fundamentally individualistic, moral and volitional. The belief is that the appeal to the good intentions of each individual can transform society. And, indeed, this is precisely the appeal which Wesley himself made.

The contemporary world is, however, quite different from that of Wesley. Society is now dominated by gargantuan corporate institutions, an all-pervasive mass media and a technology predicated on efficiency and utility. The great challenge of Marxism lies in its assertion that evil is located not only in individual hearts and minds, but also in society itself – in its corporate and class structures and methods of production. The question then is: Can society be transformed without a thorough understanding of the nature of this kind of evil? And are there forces in the modern world which in and of themselves overwhelm individual effort and render it impotent? In particular, does the modern phenomenon of technology which dominates the means of production so govern the totality of our lives that it leaves no room for individual responsibility?

Coulson was not unaware of these questions and in his Pegram lectures and his lecture on responsibility at Heriot-Watt University he spoke of the political problems raised by large-scale science. But he never departed from his belief that responsibility was an individual matter; if we all behaved responsibly then science could be controlled and used beneficially. And when he spoke of technology he always linked it with science in a way that implied that it posed problems which were not different in kind from those of science. There are those, however, who dispute that individual responsibility is meaningful in the modern context. They argue that the fusion of science and technology has created not only an entirely new situation but one in which we have lost control of our destiny. There is no doubt that had Coulson lived he would have engaged in further discussion of this question. The finest tribute that we can give to his memory is to continue to wrestle with such questions with the same honesty and integrity he showed both in his life and in his thought.

Appendix A

Modern Cosmology and Some of its Implications

In the last quarter of a century our understanding of the universe has been changed by the information which modern space technology has afforded us[1] and by new developments in theoretical physics. What are some of the implications of this new understanding in modern cosmology?

We have already noted in chapter 2 that modern cosmology points to a universe of simply immense proportions. Our earth is only one of a series of planets orbiting a perfectly ordinary sun. Our sun is itself one of perhaps a thousand million. The galaxy to which we belong is approximately 100,000 light years across, and is only one of many.[2] These galaxies are separated by vast distances – up to 1,000 million light years. This immense universe is also very old. Estimates about its age vary somewhat, but it would appear to be in the order of 10–15,000 million years old, while the age of the earth is estimated at around 5,000 million years. The human race is thought to be about one million years old. Some Christians find this very disconcerting, but not so Coulson. He often recounted how he was taken to task after one of his lectures by a Russian scientist who found it incredible that a scientist could also be a Christian. He asked Coulson how he explained that the universe and the earth were around for so long before humans came on the scene. Even if we were to assume that there was a God, did this not indicate that humans were rather insignificant in his plan? Coulson's reply was indicative not only of his gracious manner but also of his perspicacity. He acknowledged that the question was a good one, and then went on to say that it did not at all indicate that humans were unimportant in God's plan, but rather indicated that God 'valued nature for itself, and found some means of satisfaction in it, independent of man's later existence'.[3] This is a most significant point by Coulson, and we have seen that it was one to which he returned many times in his writings. God delights in the physical world, which is valuable in its own right.

Today, however, there is another way of answering the Russian's question. Contemporary theoretical physicists have come to the conclusion that the vast size and age of the universe is absolutely necessary for there to be any life at all. As Polkinghorne explains:

> The reason for the necessary size is that a world much smaller would have run its course before life had time to appear. It takes about 18,000 million years to make men, both because the evolution of complex life takes time and also because it can only get going at all in the second generation of stars and planets. This realization gives a surprising twist to our contemplation of the immensity of the universe. Without all those trillions and trillions of stars we should not be here to be dismayed by them![4]

The development of radio-astronomy has enabled us to 'see' more clearly not only the stars in our own galaxy, but also other galaxies. These galaxies are seen to be in motion, some spiralling around their centre as they move through space. It has also been observed that every galaxy appears to be moving away from every other galaxy, and the rate of recession from us is almost directly proportional to its distance away – that is, the galaxies nearer to us are receding at a slower rate than those further away.[5] Eddington's analogy of the balloon is useful in trying to explain what this means. Dots are placed on a partially inflated balloon at uniform and regular intervals. The balloon is then blown up further and as the diameter expands every dot gets further away from every other dot, but the rate of separation is greatest for those dots which are furthest apart on the sphere.[6] If we let the air out of the balloon, then of course it contracts and the dots eventually merge into each other. So it is believed also that there was a time when all the galaxies were compressed into one 'point', or 'singularity' as the theoretical physicists call it. This was the beginning of the universe as we know it.

If we say that all the galaxies were originally one, how exactly are we to picture this original state? Thirty-five years ago many scientists agreed with Lemaître who thought that all the matter in the universe was the result of a primeval explosion of unimaginable force. This has become known as the big bang, the moment of creation, and explains why the galaxies are still receding from one another.

There was considerable discussion among Coulson's contemporaries about whether the universe did begin with a big bang.[7] Scientists such as Fred Hoyle argued that there was insufficient scientific evidence to enable us to speak meaningfully about a beginning to the universe. He maintained, moreover, that new stars were continually being created. He contended that as galaxies and stars move through the hydrogen 'fog' of space they suck in hydrogen atoms through the attraction of their gravitational fields. Thus galaxies and stars are constantly adding hydrogen to their nuclear fires. Quite small lumps of matter will attract hydrogen atoms, and these eventually (over millions of years!) will form new stars. Scientists have found ways of estimating the age of stars and have found some to be younger than others. This was only explicable, claimed Hoyle, if there was continuous development.[8]

The continuous creation theory has in recent years been almost universally abandoned by cosmologists and theoretical physicists and most of them now believe that the universe did have a beginning. At the beginning of time all matter was compressed into one singularity. This singularity exploded with unimaginable force to give rise eventually to the universe as we know it. Exactly how this explosion and subsequent expansion came about, however, is still not clear. Theoretical physicists such as Alan Guth of MIT have modified the big bang theory by positing a 'super-cooling'[9] stage after the initial explosion. In this supercooled state a 'false vacuum' is created in which the phenomenon of gravitational repulsion 'inflates' the universe so that it explodes at a speed faster than in the standard big bang theory. The details of the argument are very technical[10] but one of the attractions of Guth's theory for theoretical physicists is that it explains how the universe could have started from almost nothing – from compressed matter weighing about ten kilos – about the same as a well-packed bag of groceries. This led Guth to make his well-known remark that the universe was 'the ultimate free lunch'.

Guth's ideas explain other very puzzling features of the universe: why, for example, its mass density was so exactly right that it produced a universe in which human life was possible. The early explosion required remarkable 'fine tuning' to produce the present universe. The odds against the universe turning out as it did by chance are simply enormous.[11] This has led some to posit the 'anthropic cosmological principle'.[12] In its simplest form this states that the only way to explain the universe is by our presence in it. P. C. W. Davies, in his book *The Accidental Universe*, notes that the line of reasoning involved in the anthropic principle is 'contrary to the spirit of the Copernican Revolution'. He goes on:

> Nicholas Copernicus, by denying the special status of the earth in cosmic dynamics, initiated a tradition which has influenced scientific thinking for four centuries. In most respects that earth can be regarded as most unexceptional in status, and typical of vast numbers of similar planets near similar stars in similar galaxies. Yet our existence in biological organisms has selected for us a location in space which is in some sense atypical. Although the earth may not claim special status among planets, the fact that we find ourselves living on a solid surface, when the vast majority of the material in the universe is in the form of tenuous gas clouds or balls of hot plasma, and the fact that we are located near a stable star, when many stars have erratic behaviour or are grouped in multiple systems unsuitable for equable planets, is no coincidence. We could not, presumably, survive in the hostile environment associated with more typical cosmic material. Similarly, our temporal location in the cosmos is constrained by the fact that the universe evolves, and during its evolution from a hot, dense furnace to a collection of burnt-out, dispersed galaxies, only a relatively restricted time interval is suitable for life.[13]

Some Christians have seized upon this 'principle' and think that here theoretical physics has given us a fundamental religious insight. But we should be rather wary of pushing the anthropic principle too far. In a similar vein there were Christians in Coulson's day who seized upon the idea that before the big bang there was only radiation. Does Genesis not say that the earth was without form and void, and God said, 'Let there be light!'? Light is, of course, a type of radiation, but Coulson, with his customary common sense, coun-selled against making too much of this kind of parallel between the scientific and biblical accounts of creation. As for the obvious question of where the radiation came from in the first place, Coulson notes that this is simply not a scientific question. (It is, in fact, a variant of the age-old theological question of whether God created the world *ex nihilo*.) It is not a scientific question because there is no scientific data which could be used to answer it. It is a metaphysical question, one which goes beyond an inquiry into the physical world, and therefore Coulson, as a scientist, refused to speculate about it. Similarly in the case of the anthropic principle we should be wary of drawing a metaphysical conclusion from an observation about the improbability of the universe in which we live.

Coulson thus counsels against thinking that theoretical physics could give us the answer to metaphysical questions.[14] Did God create the world? Is the existence of a universe such as ours proof that God has a purpose for humankind? These questions cannot be answered by science. But science can – and does – describe a universe of extraordinary complexity, and one in which our presence at the very least leaves a question mark.

Appendix B

Coulson's Pacifism

Coulson became a pacifist after his 'spiritual rebirth' in 1930. From that point on his pacifist beliefs were an extremely important part of his life and thought. It behoves us therefore to say something about the basis of his pacifism.

During the Second World War Coulson registered as a conscientious objector. In his statement to the tribunal which granted him this status he spelled out clearly that his pacifism was 'based on religious grounds'. As a Christian he felt he could have no part in war, and joined the Fellowship of Reconciliation and served on its London committees for many years. He was also one of the first lay members of the Methodist Peace Fellowship.

Fundamentally Coulson believed that the central teaching of Jesus could be put in two words: love and fellowship, towards God and towards humankind. A Christian must strive to love others and to seek to deepen and enrich whatever fellowship there is. Love implies a deep respect for others, so that we must treat them as human beings for whom Christ died; and fellowship implies a sharing of activity and possession, so that we may never exploit our neighbours nor rejoice at their misfortune. Coulson believed that not only were both of these characteristics in the life and teaching of Jesus, but that the history of the early church showed their power to redeem evil and transform the evil-doer. Warfare was, however, a denial of love and fellowship. One cannot love those whom one maims and kills, and the hate and brutality which are engendered by warfare are destructive of all human fellowship. Thus Coulson considered that if he were to be a Christian he had to be a pacifist.

There are, of course, all kinds of reasons why people become pacifists, and Coulson knew this well enough. Some argue that war makes no economic sense. As a nation's resources become gobbled up by increasing military expenditure, less money is available for the housing, health and education of its citizens. Others put the case slightly differently and claim that war makes no political sense. Modern warfare is so destructive both to the victor and the defeated that it is hard to see what possible political objectives could be gained through it. But Coulson did not think that either economic or political arguments were enough to carry the pacifist case.

Coulson was more impressed by scientific arguments which were used to support the pacifist position. By the early 1970s, for example, science had provided us with a great deal of information about the possible effects of a nuclear war. It would devastate the earth. Since Coulson's death such chilling books as Jonathan Schell's *The Fate of the Earth*[1] have stressed that the devastation would be total and the earth would be left uninhabitable. Computer-assisted studies done by Carl Sagan and other scientists on the 'nuclear winter' which would follow a war have also painted a similar picture. It is a truly terrifying prospect. Yet the fear of a nuclear holocaust does not in and of itself make people pacifists. Opinion polls consistently show that people will not elect a party to government which pledges to give up nuclear weapons. The public knows the risks involved with nuclear weapons, but still does not want to abandon them. Coulson recognized the reality of this and acknowledged that simple fear of a holocaust was no basis on which to build peace. The most that could be achieved by such fear is an absence of war. But mere absence of war, says Coulson, is not what a Christian means by peace.

Coulson's pacifism is, then, deeply religious. Since he saw science as a religious activity it is no surprise that he thought it could contribute to the quest for peace. This comes out most clearly in a statement he made at a symposium on atomic warfare:

> I have spoken of science as universal, and of the moral outrage on its tradition when we indulge in war. But those of us who are Christians will be able to carry the argument a stage further. Science acquires its universal character from the fact that it is a revelation of God, before whom all the peoples of the earth are as one family. Here indeed is the ground of our objection not only to atomic warfare, but to all war – that it does despite to the true stature of man as a child of God – that it infringes the essential unity of mankind, concerning which Tolstoy said that it was the most important thing about the human race. Science, we believe, is rooted in a religious experience and a religious conviction,

whether it be recognized as such, or not: and its sanctions are essentially religious sanctions, whether they be put in conventional religious terms or not . . . [Both] from the nature of science and the structure of human living, all warfare is [seen to be] immoral.[2]

Coulson had thought through his pacifism very carefully. He knew that the rock on which it was founded was his own personal experience of faith, but he also recognized that there were certain social implications which followed from it. It is not enough to renounce war and do nothing about its causes. He saw quite clearly that an 'equitable sharing of the world's resources is an essential adjunct to peace'. His pacifism was not just a privately held conviction, but part of his social conscience, and one of the reasons he devoted so much time and energy to organizations such as Oxfam.

There are two major objections which may be brought against a pacifist position such as Coulson's, and he was aware of them both. In the first place there is the objection that pacifism is not integral to Christian belief. Coulson's response to this was to point out that the 'ultimate reaction of the very early Christians was pacifist'. He went on:

The riposte that our Lord drove the money lenders out of the Temple is no adequate reply to this. For apart from Cornelius and one or two others at Caesarea, and the gaoler who was baptized by Peter at Philippi, there is no direct evidence of any Christian as a soldier until after AD 170. Furthermore, Celsus, the earliest literary opponent of Christians, reproached them (c. AD 178) for being un-Roman, unpatriotic and unwilling to render military service to the emperor (how modern this sounds!). Tertullian of Carthage (c. AD 200) compliments a soldier on being martyred for refusal to fight. Origen, the greatest theologian of the first half of the third century, says that the wars of the Old Testament were allegorical: 'We Christians no longer take up sword against nation, having become children of peace, for the sake of Jesus.'[3]

The great change came after the conversion of Constantine in AD 312 and the recognition of Christianity as a state religion in AD 324. Constantine thought that God had helped him in battle, and we find the Council of Arles (AD 314) making the decree that 'they who throw away their weapons in time of peace shall be excommunicated'. This was a complete volte-face, but one predicated not on some new theological insight, but rather on the changed status of Christianity from a private to a state religion. From Augustine onwards it became common for theologians to defend Christian involvement with war. This Coulson believed to have been a development which was fundamentally at odds with earliest Christianity.

The second objection to pacifism is that in the kind of society in which we live it is impossible to practise it. It often takes the pointed form of asking a question such as: What would you do if someone tried to rape your wife? Pacifists usually respond to this argument by differentiating between individual personal violence and war. Coulson himself argued for this distinction, but did recognize that it was not always an easy one to make. There are some situations in which the line between the two is not easily drawn. Pacifists have to recognize that there may be situations which are very difficult. Coulson found himself in just such a situation, which he related thus:

> I happened to be in Malaya some fifteen years ago [i.e. 1954] at the time of the communist guerilla activity: and I narrowly missed being ambushed when going from Kuala Lumpur to Singapore. The car which followed me was caught; I was lucky. This was one of those situations where, if I had been in command, I should not have known what was right. It was clearly not large-scale war. Nor was it a case of one man coming to rape my wife. If it had been the former I should have refused to fight; if it had been the latter I should not have hesitated more than a moment before letting fly with all the strength in my arms, trying to knock out my opponent. In the case of war I cannot deal with the individual opponent: in the case of my wife's attacker I can. If I drop an atomic bomb on the country with whom I am at war, there is no time for forgiveness, or a change of heart; but if I deal with the person coming toward my wife there is at least the possibility that by dealing directly with him I may give the grace of God a chance to lead him (perhaps through me) to repentance. War spoils human relationships and denies the brotherhood of man . . . I can take no part in it. But there are situations, such as the difficult one I described in Malaya, where I do not yet see so clearly.[4]

Coulson's pacifism, then, was deeply felt and clearly thought out. He himself summarized his position thus:

> We should not argue for our pacifism because now it is too expensive to fight, or because it is not politically expedient to

fight, or because too many million people would be killed if we fight, or because an atomic bomb is not a very pleasant thing, and you risk such things if you do fight. These may all be true, but they do not go to the heart of the matter: they are a bit of the shading in the picture, and not the picture itself. The picture itself for me is what it was on the day that I became a Christian. 'This is not the way our Lord taught us to live with one another' was my personal and spontaneous conviction about the ways of war.[5]

Appendix C

Coulson's Non-Scientific Writings and Lectures

Books and Pamphlets

Contributions of Science to Peace (Alex Wood Memorial Lecture), Fellowship of Reconciliation 1953

Christianity in an Age of Science (Riddell Memorial Lectures), Oxford University Press 1953

Science and Religion – a Changing Relationship (Rede Lecture), Cambridge University Press 1955

Science and Christian Belief (John Calvin McNair Lectures), Oxford University Press and University of North Carolina Press 1955 and Fontana Books 1958

Some Problems of the Atomic Age (Scott Lidgett Memorial Lecture), Epworth Press 1957.

Nuclear Knowledge and Christian Responsibilities, Epworth Press 1958

Science and the Idea of God (Eddington Memorial Lecture), Cambridge University Press 1958

Finding God in Science, The Upper Room, Tennessee 1959

Science, Technology and the Christian (The Beckly Social Service Lecture), Epworth Press 1960, Abingdon Press 1961 and Greenwood Press 1978.

Science Tells Us – How Much?, SPCK 1961

The Church in the World (Peter Ainslie Memorial Lecture), Rhodes University, Grahamstown 1962

Responsibility (Tawney Memorial Lecture), CSM 1966

Faith and Technology (Inaugural Lecture, Luton Industrial College), Chester House Publications 1969

The Scientist's Responsibility in Society, Heriot-Watt University 1970

Articles

'The Christian Religion and Contemporary Science', *Modern Churchman* 40, 1950, pp. 205–15

'The Place of Science as a Cohesive Force in Modern Society', *Dublin Review* 225, 1951, pp. 49–59

'The Place of Science in the Christian Faith', *Church Pastoral-Aid Society Fellowship Paper* 13 (no. 156), 1951

'Science and Religion' (BBC broadcast discussion with I. T. Ramsey), *Church Pastoral-Aid Fellowship Paper* 13 (no. 149), 1951

'Atomic Energy: The Moral Issue', *Biological Hazards of Atomic Energy* ed. A. Haddow, Clarendon Press 1952, pp. 215–19

'The Unity of Science and Faith', *Christianity in an Age of Science*, Canadian Broadcasting Corporation, Toronto 1952, pp. 41–9

'God the Creator', *Church of England Youth Council Newsletter* 1, 1952, pp. 3–15

'The Longing for Truth', *Question* 6, 1953, pp. 26–45

'The Way to God through Science', *Ways to God* ed. C. E. Raven et al., The Layman Publishing Co. 1954, pp. 16–19

'The Use and Abuse of Science', *Preacher's Quarterly* 1, 1954, pp. 30–5

'Science and Religion', *Advancement of Science* 11, 1954, pp. 321–32

Contribution to Symposium on the Morality of Atomic Warfare, *Atomic Scientists Journal* 4, 1954, pp. 8–11

'Science and Religion', *Main Currents in Modern Thought* 11, 1955, pp. 103–7

'The Scientific Method and Human Relations', *Manager* 24, 1956, pp. 69–74

'Science as Part of our Culture', *Journal of the Association of Assistant Mistresses* 7, 1956, pp. 25–32

'The Natural Sciences', *An Approach to Christian Education* ed. Rupert E. Davies, Epworth Press 1956, pp. 41–57

'Case History in Hell', *Preacher's Quarterly* 2, 1956, pp. 41–6

'Living in an Atomic Age', *Birmingham Teachers Journal* 8, 1956, pp. 13–18

'The Age of Nuclear Power', *Ordnance* 41, 1957, pp. 978–80

'Science and the Preacher', *Preacher's Handbook* ed. Greville P. Lewis, Epworth Press 1957, pp. 1–11

'The Christian and the Atom', *New Christian Advocate*, 1957, pp. 42–6

'The Atomic Age and Christian Responsibility', *Presbyterian Leader*, July 1957, pp. 107–10

'Scientific Development and Christianity', *Focus* 2, May 1957, pp. 3–5 (part I); June 1957, pp. 3–6 (part II)

'Science and Religion', *St Martin's Review* 797, 1957, pp. 237–40; 798, pp. 269–72; 799, pp. 300–4

'Science and Christianity', *World Christian Digest* 103, 1957, pp. 5–11

'The Modern World and the Gospel of Christ', *God's Good News*, Methodist Evangelistic Materials (Washington) 1958, pp. 97–112

'God the Creator', *Steps to Christian Understanding* ed. R. J. W. Bevan, Oxford University Press 1958, pp. 50–70

'Science and Technology in the Twentieth Century', *Report of Conference of Science Teachers*, Oxford Institute of Education 1959, pp. 19–23

'Some Recent Developments in Science and their Implications for Theology', *London Quarterly and Holborn Review* July 1959, pp. 176–88

'The Changing Relationship of Science and Religion', *London Quarterly and Holborn Review* October 1959, pp. 280–3

'Life or Death', *A New Age for Peace* ed. L. MacLachlan, Fellowship of Reconciliation 1959, pp. 40–1

'Life in a Test Tube – so what?', *Youth* July–August 1959, pp. 5–8

'The Modern World and the Gospel of Christ', *Methodist Layman* 19, 1959, pp. 2–11

'Fact and Fiction in Physics', *Bulletin of the Malayan Mathematical Society* 6, 1959, pp. 61–8

'Likes and Dislikes in Mathematics', *Bulletin of the Malayan Mathematical Society* 6, 1959, pp. 29–35

'Some Problems of the Atomic Age', *London Churchman* 11, 1959, pp. 5–7

'Christ Confronts our Age – the "age of science"', *Prophets for Our World* (sermons at St Aldate's Oxford) ed. Keith de Berry et al., Mowbray 1960, pp. 69–79

'Fact and Fiction in Physics', *Bucknell Review* 9, 1960, pp. 1–14

'As a Scientist I am sure that Life must go on', *Is there Life after Death?* Arthur James Press 1960, pp. 19–26

'Protestant Thought and Natural Science: A Review Article on *Protestant Thought and Natural Science* by John Dillenberger', *Drew Gateway* 31, 1961, pp. 107–11

'Science and Religion', *Crane Review* 4, 1961, pp. 32–51

'The Methodist Doctrine of Perfect Love', *Proceedings of the Tenth World Methodist Conference* ed. E. Benson Perkins and Elmer T. Clark, Epworth Press 1961, pp. 281–5

'Mathematics and the Real World', *Calcutta Mathematical Society Golden Jubilee Commemoration Volume* 1958–59, pp. 261–9

'A Secular World? – God and "Things"', *Laity* 16, 1963, pp. 31–7

'A Scientist's View of the Honest-to-God Debate', *Impetus* 35, 1966, pp. 35–43

'Science and Religion', *Proceedings of the Royal Institution of Great Britain* 41, 1967, pp. 480–92

'Commitment', *Three Views on Commitment* ed. Lord Caradon et al., Longman 1967, pp. 26–56

'Miracles and Visions', *Asking Them Questions* Vol. I ed. R. Selby Wright, Oxford University Press 1972, pp. 79–89

Minor Works

'All or Nothing', review article of J. Bronowski's *The Common Sense of Science* in *Religion in Education* 1951, pp. 25–8

'Science and Religion in Partnership', *Life and Work* 1951, pp. 183–4

'A Christian Sermon', *Scouter*, December 1952, p. 254–5

'Science and Religion', review article of Karl Heim's *Faith and The Scientific Attitude*, *View Review* 1953, pp. 18–20

'How Old is the Universe?', *Listener* 1953, pp. 90–2

'Science and Religion', *Daystar* 1954, pp. 16–18

'Christianity and the Scientist', *Cherwell*, 18 October 1955, p. 4

'Building a New World' (Address to Methodist Conference), *Reconciliation*, November 1954

'Ban Big Scale Atomic Bomb Tests?' *Together*, November 1956, pp. 16–18

'You and the H-bomb', *Rally*, May 1957, pp. 4–6

'Born for this Hour', *Cannock Chase* 34, March 1958, pp. 1–2

'Facts – Some of the Data', *Prism* 2, September 1958, pp. 11–12

'What is Twentieth Century Opportunity?' *Layman* 9, September 1959, pp. 252–3

'A Ciencia e a fé', *Portugal Evangelico* 40, November 1959, pp. 1–2

'Greetings from the Vice-President', *Over to You* 13, 1959, p. 4

'Are We outgrowing Religion?', *The Christian Replies* ed. Leslie Dawson, Epworth Press 1960, p. 19

'God's Whole World', *Exeter Circuit Quarterly Bulletin*, April/June 1960, p. 1

'New Year Message', *Joyful News*, 7 January 1960, p. 1

'Science – Is it Friend or Foe?', *Methodist News*, January 1960, p. 2

'But Charles Darwin did not deny a Creator', *Vanguard*, February 1960, pp. 21–2

'Optimist or Pessimist?', *Irish Advocate*, 15 July 1960, p. 4

'Some Problems of the Atomic Age', *London Churchman*, February 1960, pp. 5–7

'Moral Responsibilities in a Scientific Age', *Livingstonian*, 2 October 1961, pp. 19–22

'The Work of the Layman', *Vatican Council* (Special Bulletin) 31, 1962, pp. 255–6

'The University as a Promised Land', *Light and Salt Periodical* 1, Autumn 1962, p. 2–7

'The Earth is the Lord's, *Christian Education* 21, November 1962, pp. 49–50

'Is God Dead?', *Science Review* 19, 1964, pp. 68–70

'Both Timid and Generous – a Comment on the Vatican II Decree on the Apostolate of the Laity', *Bulletin of the Department on the Laity* (World Council of Churches), 1966, pp. 40–1

'1983–85', *Conference Speeches given at the Association of Head Mistresses' Conference* 1966, pp. 55–68

'Luther and Science', *Methodist Recorder*, 23 September 1967

'Human Nature and Moral Rule', *New Christian*, 18 April 1968, p. 11

'Old and New in the Twentieth Century', *Outlook*, 2 June 1966, pp. 22–3

'The Role of Science in Developing Countries', *Zenith*, August 1971

'Live Easily as Leaves grow on the Tree', *P.H.P. International Magazine* (Japan), 1972, p. 31

Book Reviews

Reviews of:

L. E. Browne, *Where Science and Religion Meet*, 1950, in *View-Review*

A. Einstein, *Out of my later Years*, 1950, in *British Journal of the Philosophy of Science* (*BJPhilSc*)

E. Schrödinger, *Science and Humanism*, 1951, in *Science Progress*

J. L. Synge, *Science: Sense and Nonsense*, 1951, in *BJPhilSc*

G. E. Quinton, *Scientific and Religious Knowledge*, 1951, in *View-Review*

G. D. Yarnold, *Christianity and Physical Science*, 1951, in *View-Review*

H. Dingle, *The Scientific Adventure*, 1952, in *BJPhilSc* and *Modern Free Churchman*

N. Wiener, *The Human Use of Human Beings*, 1952, in *BJPhilSc*

Homer W. Smith, *Man and his Gods*, 1953, in *Methodist Recorder*

C. E. Raven, *Science and Religion – A New Interpretation of their Relationship*, 1953, in *Methodist Recorder*

G. D. Yarnold, *God's World*, 1953, in *View-Review*

Mary B. Hesse, *Science and the Human Imagination: Aspects of the History and Logic of Physical Science*, 1954, in *Nature*

A. R. Smethurst, *Modern Science and Christian Beliefs*, 1955, in *Methodist Recorder*

R. O. Kapp, *Facts and Faith*, 1955, in *Science Progress*

A. Trafford, *Science and the Great Design*, 1955, in *Methodist Recorder*

G. Thompson, *The Foreseeable Future*, 1955, in *Oxford Times*

M. Hachiya, *Hiroshima Diary*, 1955, in *Reconciliation*

E. J. Russell, *Science and Modern Life*, 1955, in *Oxford Mail*

R. Calder, *Science Makes Sense*, 1955, in *Methodist Recorder*

E. W. Sinnott, *The Biology of the Spirit*, 1955, in *Scientific Monthly*

G. R. Harrison, *What Man May Be – the Human Side of Science*, 1957, in *Nature*

R. Hooykaas, *Christian Faith and the Freedom of Science*, 1957, in *New Scientist*

D. Lack, *Evolutionary Theory and Christian Belief: The Unresolved Conflict*, 1957, in *Endeavour*

J. A. V. Butler, *Science and Human Life*, 1957, in *New Scientist*

J. Huxley, *Religion without Revelation*, 1957, in *New Scientist*

J. Russell, *Science and Metaphysics*, 1959, in *New Scientist*

P. Fothergill, *Life and its Origin*, 1959, in *New Scientist*

L. Bright, *Whitehead's Philosophy of Physics*, 1959, in *New Scientist*

M. Polanyi, *Personal Knowledge*, 1959, in *Hibbert Journal*

A. N. Gilkes, *Faith for Modern Man*, 1960, *View-Review*

R. E. D. Clark, *Christian Belief and Science*, 1960, in *View-Review*

W. Stein (ed), *Nuclear Weapons and Christian Conscience*, 1961, in *Methodist Recorder*

L. Eiseley, *The Firmament of Time*, 1961, in *Methodist Recorder*

B. Russell, *Fact and Fiction*, 1962, in *Methodist Recorder*

H. K. Schilling, *Science and Religion*, 1963, in *New Scientist*

W. R. Hindmarsh, *Science and Faith*, 1967, in *Methodist Recorder*

C. H. D. Clark, *The Scientist and the Supernatural*, 1967, in *Preacher's Quarterly*

I. G. Barbour, *Issues in Science and Religion*, 1968, in *New Scientist*

C. Lanczos, *Space through the Ages*, 1970, in *Mathematical Gazette*

G. Moores, *Mathematics and Religion – Two Languages*, 1970, in *Mathematical Gazette*

R. E. D. Clark, *Science and Christianity: A Partnership*, 1973, in *Nature*

Public and Invitational Lectures

Riddell Lectures, Newcastle, 1953: 'Christianity in an Age of Science'

Rede Lecture, Cambridge, 1954: 'Science and Religion – a Changing Relationship'

John Calvin McNair Lectures, Chapel Hill, USA, 1954: 'Science and Christian Belief'

SCM Lectures, Manchester University, 1956: 'Science and the Christian' (unpublished)

Firth Lectures, Nottingham, 1957: 'Christian Belief in the Modern World' (unpublished)

Second Scott Lidgett Lecture, 1957: 'Some Problems of the Atomic Age'

Eleventh Arthur Stanley Eddington Lecture, Cambridge, 1958: 'Science and the Idea of God'

Beckly Lectures, 1960: 'Science, Technology and the Christian'

George B. Pegram Lectures, Brookhaven, USA, 1962: 'The Scientist and Society' (unpublished)

Peter Ainslie Memorial Lecture, Rhodes University, South Africa, 1962: 'The Church in the World'

Second Tawney Lecture, 1965: 'Responsibility'

Sir D. Owen Evans Lectures, Aberystwyth, 1966: 'The Influence of Science on the Christian Faith' (unpublished)

Freemantle Lectures, Oxford, 1968: 'Science and Faith' (unpublished)

Abbreviations

of titles of Coulson's works referred to in the notes

'Commitment'	'Commitment' in *Three Views on Commitment* ed. Lord Caradon, C. A. Coulson and T. Huddleston, Longman 1967, pp. 26–56
CAS	*Christianity in an Age of Science*, Oxford University Press 1953
FT	*Faith and Technology*, The Upper Room, 1971
'Natural Sciences'	'The Natural Sciences' in *An Approach to Religious Education*, ed. Rupert E. Davies, Epworth Press 1956, pp. 41–57
Nuclear Knowledge	*Nuclear Knowledge and Christian Responsibilities*, Epworth Press 1958
PAA	*Some Problems of the Atomic Age*, Epworth Press 1960
Responsibility	*Responsibility*, CSM 1966
SCB	*Science and Christian Belief*, Oxford University Press 1955
ScF	'Science and Faith: A Changing Relationship', unpublished lecture given in Canterbury in 1970
ScR	*Science and Religion: A Changing Relationship*, Cambridge University Press 1955
SIG	*Science and the Idea of God*, Cambridge University Press 1958
SRS	*The Scientist's Responsibility in Society*, Heriot-Watt University 1970
STC	*Science, Technology and the Christian*, Epworth Press 1960

Notes

1 Charles Alfred Coulson

1. We are grateful to Mrs Eileen Coulson and Andrew Coulson for the helpful information they gave us when we were writing this chapter. See S. L. Altmann and E. J. Bowen, *Biographical Memoirs of Fellows of the Royal Society* 20, 1974, pp. 73–134, for a good account of Coulson's life.

2. The formation of the first Group is described in *A Group Speaks*, Epworth Press 1931.

3. Coulson even showed an interest in meteorology. His very first published paper was on geostrophic winds and corrected an aspect of the work of Sir Harold Jeffreys, the famous meteorologist.

4. *Waves*, Oliver & Boyd 1941, [2]1943, [3]1944, [4]1947, [5]1949, [6]1952, [7]1955, reprinted 1958, 1961, 1965; *Electricity*, Oliver and Boyd 1948, [2]1951, [3]1953, [4]1956, [5]1958 reprinted 1961, 1965; *Valence*, Clarendon Press 1952, reprinted Oxford University Press 1961, 1965; *The Shape and Structure of Molecules*, Clarendon Press 1973. Coulson also co-authored *A Dictionary of pi-calculations*, Pergamon Press 1968.

5. These are only a few of the committees Coulson served on. A complete list is found among his papers deposited in the Bodleian Library, Oxford.

6. See Appendix C.

2 Faith and The Challenge of Science

1. It is worth noting that Copernicus had found the heliocentric hypothesis in ancient Greek writers – not all of them agreed with Aristotle.

2. James Ussher (1581–1656) was Archbishop of Armagh. A distinguished scholar in his day, he is now remembered chiefly for his dating of the beginning of creation in 4004 BC.

3. There are those who argue, of course, that significance has nothing to do with size – see, for example, the famous comment of John A. Baker in *The Foolishness of God*, Darton, Longman and Todd 1978, p. 53 on the argument that the size of the universe means we are insignificant and unimportant: 'This small anthropocentric criticism is not an argument. It is nothing more than the complaining voice of mean, utilitarian, gutless, heartless, cerebral, twentieth-century, profit margin, Western man.'

4. Quoted from the first of a series of unpublished lectures, 'Science and

the Christian', p. 3, delivered in 1956 at Manchester University under the auspices of the SCM. The typescript of these lectures is found among Coulson's collected papers in the Bodleian Library in Oxford.

5. Coulson expands upon this point in *ScR*, pp. 19–21.

6. 'Science and the Christian', p. 8.

7. Ibid., p. 9. Note in a similar vein Coulson's article 'God the Creator' in *Steps to Christian Understanding*, ed. R. J. W. Bevan, Oxford University Press 1958, p. 62: 'For we hold a doctrine of creation, and believe that creation, whatever it was, was an act of God. The doctrine itself is an attempt to express our conviction that the very galaxies are the product of his power and wisdom. And what power! The enormous space and the unthinkable energy are *his* space, *his* energy.' (Note that in this and all subsequent quotations the emphases are always those of the author himself.)

8. 'Science and the Christian', p. 9.

9. In his latter years Coulson made a number of statements which suggest a certain ambiguity in his thinking on this point. These statements were, however, made in lectures which were never published. In, for example, the fourth of his Freemantle Lectures given at Balliol College in 1968, he stated that 'man was quite possibly a passing phenomenon on the stage of universal history'. He echoed this sentiment in a lecture 'What is a Human Being?' given in Australia in 1969. But if the human race, which 'completes' God's plan, dies out, what happens to the plan?

10. 'Science and the Christian', p. 10.

11. Ibid., p. 11.

12. Quoted in *SCB*, p. 101.

13. This is a saying of Einstein's which is found in German carved above a fireplace in Fine Hall, Princeton. Quoted by Coulson in *SCB*, p. 61.

14. 'Science and the Christian', p. 14.

15. Ibid., p. 30.

16. See 'Darwin's Origin of Species', *Quarterly Review* 108, 1860, pp. 225–64. Wilberforce's authorship of this article was not made public until it was reprinted in his *Essays Contributed to the Quarterly Review*, London 1874.

17. Cf. also 'God the Creator', p. 53: 'Fred Hoyle . . . [has] said that 'Man's unguided imagination could never have chanced on such a structure. No literary genius could have invented a story one-hundredth part as fantastic as the sober facts unearthed by astronomical science.' For Hoyle's latest (and basically similar) views see his *The Intelligent Universe*, Michael Joseph 1983.

18. In view of what Coulson says here it is perhaps a little ironic that he was awarded the Lecomte du Nouy prize in 1956 for his book *Science and Christian Belief*.

19. P. Lecomte du Nouy, *Human Destiny*, Longman 1947, p. 36.

20. The second Sir D. Owen Evans lecture, p. 8.

21. The example is taken from David Lack, *Evolutionary Theory and Christian Belief*, Methuen 1957.

22. In this connection it is noteworthy that Peter Alexander makes such a criticism in his review of Coulson's *Science and Christian Belief* in the *British Journal of the Philosophy of Science* 8, 1958, pp. 76f. Subsequently Coulson

was always very careful to stress that he was arguing by analogy, and not trying to provide some epistemological basis for the unity of science and religion.

23. The second of the Sir D. Owen Evans Lectures, p. 10. Coulson put the argument slightly differently in 'God the Creator', p. 51: 'I myself believe that there are certain insights which are given to those of us who are professional scientists (just as, of course, there are other insights given to the artist, and the poet and the ordinary simple Christian) which are not given to anyone else, and without which, therefore, the total life of the community is impoverished. That, incidentally, is why the scientist must be given complete and unqualified freedom to explore and experiment; that is why it is so important, in the name of holy living, that no theologian, or politician, or anybody else, should attempt in any way to impose restrictions on this work.'

It is interesting to note here that Coulson himself was a pacifist who refused invitations to work on the atomic bomb during and after the Second World War. Is there not some inconsistency in publicly proclaiming that there should be no restrictions on the work of scientists and yet privately making a decision which implies that at least some scientific enterprises should not be undertaken? See our comments in chapter 6 on Coulson's individualistic ethic.

24. Cf. the following remark by Darwin in *The Nature of Belief*, Centenary Press 1943, p. 41: 'But then arises the doubt, can the mind of man, which has, as I fully believe, been developed from a mind as low as that possessed by the lowest animal, be trusted when it draws such grand conclusions?' Quoted by Coulson in *SIG*, p. 37.

25. Stephen Hawking, in his inaugural lecture as Lucasian Professor of Mathematics at Cambridge in 1980, concluded his address, 'Is the End in Sight for Theoretical Physics?', with the following words: 'To end on a slightly alarmist note, they [theoretical physicists] may not have much more time than that [i.e. twenty years]. At present, computers are a useful aid in research, but they have to be directed by human minds. However, if one extrapolates their recent rapid rate of development, it would seem possible that they will take over altogether in theoretical physics. So maybe the end is in sight for theoretical physicists if not for theoretical physics.'

26. The second Sir D. Owen Evans lecture, p. 13.

3   The Relationship between Science and Religion

1. *Modern Churchman* 40, 1950, pp. 205–15.

2. *Dublin Review* 225, 1951, pp. 49–59.

3. The John Calvin McNair Lectures were founded through a bequest made by the Revd John Calvin McNair to the University of Chapel Hill, North Carolina. The bequest directed that 'some scientific gentleman' should deliver a course of lectures, the object of which shall be 'to show the mutual bearing of science and theology on each other, and to prove the existence and attributes, as far as may be, of God from nature'.

4. Archbishop Temple, quoted in *SCB*, p. 61.

5. Quoted in *SCB*, p. 10.

6. Quoted in *SCB*, p. 7.

7. *SCB*, p. 15.

8. *CAS*, p. 6.

9. For example, Faraday refused to work on the development of toxic chemicals for use in warfare.

10. Quoted in *CAS*, p. 8.

11. *SIG*, p. 13.

12. *SIG*, p. 16.

13. *SIG*, p. 14.

14. John C. Polkinghorne, *One World: The Interaction of Science and Theology*, SPCK 1986, p. 5.

15. Ibid., p. 108.

16. See the fascinating description of these attempts in John C. Polkinghorne, *The Quantum World*, Penguin Books 1986, pp. 53–5.

17. This view is discussed in Polkinghorne, *Quantum World*, pp. 55–8. For a comment by a non-scientist see Don Cupitt, *The Worlds of Science and Religion*, Sheldon Press 1976, pp. 58ff.

18. Polkinghorne, *Quantum World*, p. 56.

19. See Polkinghorne, *One World*, pp. 10–12.

20. A. Whitehouse, *Christian Faith and the Scientific Attitude*, Oliver and Boyd 1952, p. 121.

21. W. G. Pollard, *Chance and Providence*, Scribner 1958 and Faber 1959. For a detailed analysis of Pollard's work see D. J. Bartholomew, *God of Chance*, SCM Press 1984, pp. 125–33.

22. *SCB*, p. 21.

23. *SCB*, pp. 24–5.

24. See, for example, Hugh Montefiore, *The Probability of God*, SCM Press 1985.

25. See especially Pierre Teilhard de Chardin, *Phenomenon of Man*, Collins 1959.

26. Jacques Monod, *Chance and Necessity*, Collins 1972.

27. See above, n. 21.

28. C. E. Raven, *Experience and Interpretation*, Cambridge University Press 1953, p. 137.

29. *SIG*, pp. 15–16. The five distinct events include 'the size of the egg, which must match the size of the hedge-sparrow's or meadow pipit's in whose nest it is deposited; the delicate timing so that baby cookoo shall hatch out about thirty-six hours before the other birds; the period of incubation which requires the egg to be deposited before the foster-parent begins to sit; the physical structure necessary to eject the other occupants of the nest, and a knowledge of technique to make this ejection', ibid., p. 15.

30. David Lack, op. cit.

31. R. Dawkins, *The Blind Watchmaker*, Penguin Books 1988, p. 21. The book was originally published by Longman in 1986. It is of interest to note here that Dawkins has some harsh words for Hugh Montefiore's *The Probability of God* (see pp. 37ff.). He also criticizes Raven's argument about the parasitic way of life of the cuckoo: 'There are two things wrong with the argument put by Raven. First, there is the familiar, and I have to say rather irritating, confusion of natural selection with "randomness". Mutation is random, natural selection is the very opposite of random. Second, it just

isn't *true* that "each by itself is useless". It isn't true that the whole perfect work must have been achieved simultaneously. It isn't true that each part is essential for the success of the whole.' (p. 41).

32. *SIG*, p. 20–1.

33. A. S. Eddington, *Science and the Unseen World*, Allen and Unwin 1929, p. 43.

34. *SIG*, p. 26.

35. 'Fact and Fiction in Physics', *Bucknell Review* 9, 1960, pp. 1–14.

36. Ibid., p. 8.

37. Ibid., p. 5.

38. Ibid., p. 7.

39. *SCB*, p. 35.

40. *SCB*, p. 59.

41. *SCB*, p. 36.

42. 'Fact and Fiction in Physics, p. 13.

43. Ibid., p. 12.

44. Ibid., p. 10.

45. Ibid.

46. Ibid., p. 12.

47. Ibid., p. 11.

48. Ibid.

49. Polkinghorne, *One World*, p. 22.

50. 'Fact and Fiction in Physics', p. 10.

51. Cf. Altmann and Bowen, *Memoir*, op. cit., p. 112.

52. *CAS*, p. 39.

53. *CAS*, p. 38.

54. Polkinghorne, *One World*, pp. 22–3.

55. Ibid., p. 25.

56. 'Fact and Fiction in Physics', p. 12.

57. *CAS*, p. 19.

58. 'Science and Religion' (BBC broadcast discussion with I. T. Ramsay), *Church Pastoral-Aid Fellowship Paper* 13 (no. 149), 1951, p. 3.

59. *SCB*, pp. 84–5.

60. That reductionism is alive and well today is shown in the recent discussion of sociobiology. The debate was initiated by E. O. Wilson, whose book *Sociobiology: The New Synthesis*, Harvard University Press 1975, was aggressively reductionist. In it he suggested that the biological principles he had adumbrated should be extended to the social sciences, and evolutionary theory be applied uncompromisingly to all aspects of human existence. The work created enormous controversy. Wilson then produced a more guarded and subtle sequel, *On Human Nature*, Harvard University Press 1978, which was awarded a Pulitzer prize in 1979. But even in this work he reduced such qualities as love and altruism to genetic 'survival strategies'. See also Charles J. Lumsden and E. O. Wilson, *Genes, Mind and Culture: The Co-evolutionary Process*, Harvard University Press 1981. The best book on sociobiology is P. Kitcher, *Vaulting Ambition: Sociobiology and the Quest for Human Nature*, MIT 1985. For other discussions see *Zygon* 15, 1980, issues 3 and 4 on 'Sociobiology, Values and Religion'; *Zygon* 18, 1983, issue no. 4 on 'Origins, Functions, and Management of Aggression in

Biocultural Evolution'; *Zygon* 19, 1984, issue no. 2 on 'The Challenge of Sociobiology to Ethics and Theology'. See also A. R. Peacocke, *God and the New Biology*, especially pp. 108–15; Rada Dyson-Hudson and M. A. Little, *Rethinking Human Adaptation*, Bowker 1983; Ming T. Tsuang and R. Vandermay, *Genes and the Mind: Inheritance of Mental Illness*, Oxford University Press 1980; Donald M. Broom, *Biology of Behaviour: Mechanisms, Functions and Applications*, Cambridge University Press 1981; David A. Oakley and H. C. Plotkin, *Brain Behaviour and Evolution*, Methuen 1979; David Oakley (ed), *Brain and Mind*, Methuen 1985; John Maynard Smith (ed), *Evolution Now: A Century after Darwin*, Nature in association with Macmillan 1982.

61. *SCB*, p. 68.
62. 'Science and the Christian', lecture 2, p. 23.
63. Ibid., p. 16.
64. *SCB*, p. 71.
65. *CAS*, p. 24.
66. *CAS*, p. 44.
67. *SCB*, p. 57.
68. *SCB*, pp. 56–7.
69. *SCB*, p. 112; also *ScR*, p. 36.
70. *ScR*, p. 16.
71. *SCB*, p. 99; also *CAS*, p. 31.
72. A. R. Peacocke, *Science and the Christian Experiment*, Oxford University Press 1971. Noted by Don Cupitt, *The Worlds of Science and Religion*, p. 96.
73. *CAS*, p. 33.
74. *CAS*, p. 4. Coulson tells us of this same John Ray that his book, *The Wisdom of God Manifested in the Works of Creation*, was used by John Wesley in a shortened form in training his travelling preachers.
75. See below, appendix A.
76. *CAS*, p. 28.
77. *ScR*, p. 32.
78. *ScR*, p. 33.
79. *SCB*, p. 114.
80. Erazim Kohák, *The Embers and the Stars: A Philosophical Inquiry into the Moral Sense of Nature*, University of Chicago Press 1984, p. 45.
81. Ibid.

4   Science and Society

1. C. H. Waddington, *The Ethical Animal*, Allen and Unwin 1960, p. 13. A classic discussion of how the mediaeval 'climate of opinion' differed from ours is found in Carl L. Becker, *The Heavenly City of the Eighteenth Century Philosophers*, Yale University Press 1932, ch. 1.

2. G. P. Grant, *Philosophy in the Mass Age*, Copp Clark 1966; *Technology and Empire*, House of Anansi 1969; *Technology and Justice*, University of Notre Dame Press 1986.

3. Freeman Dyson, *Disturbing the Universe*, Harper and Row 1979, p. 7.

4. Much of this paragraph is taken from Coulson's unpublished lectures 'Science and the Christian', lecture 2, pp. 4–5.

5. Quoted in Arthur Koestler, *Heel of Achilles: Essays 1968–78*, Picador

1976, p. 30.

6. D. Morris, *The Naked Ape: A Zoologist's Study of the Human Animal*, Cape and McGraw-Hill 1967.

7. Arthur Koestler, *Arrival and Departure*, Hutchinson 1966, pp. 142–3.

8. The issue of work is significant in this context. Coulson says this was brought home to him very pointedly when he heard a minister praying in a church that he and his congregation might be saved from any hard work. Should we be aiming to abolish work? If we do, are we depriving humans of some essential aspect of human fulfilment? Although no one wants to return to the days of the Adam and Eve culture, when to live was to work, is there not a sense in which people cannot live full lives without meaningful work? These are questions which are extremely pointed when there are now so many young people who face the prospect of a life without ever having work.

9. There have been dramatic developments in computers since Coulson's day, but the illustration he gave on more than one occasion to show how computers 'learn' still has its point: 'In 1965 this machine [a computer] played the world chequers [draughts] champion, Mr W. F. Hellman. They played quickly, and the machine drew. Now that is something rather disturbing. When they played slowly, so that Mr Hellman's brain could work at a more appropriate speed, he was just able to beat it. You or I would not have had much chance. But the proprietors of the machine were not satisfied with this. They therefore put onto magnetic tape a quarter of a million complete games of chequers, played between experts. They fed these one at a time into the machine, instructing it to test whether its valuations were the best that could be, and whether, in fact, it could not learn better. This is exactly the way in which we work . . . In 1967, two years after the first chequers match, there came the following statement: "While still unable to beat the world champion in a slow game, the machine's playing ability has considerably improved." I thought of the annual reports which our children bring home from school – "his French has improved". What happened was that the machine had acquired book learning. It had learned as we learn, and had improved. Now this is a light-hearted illustration, but it will perhaps serve to reinforce the point that I am making, which is that when it comes to intellectual activity, our own constructs, our own artifacts, are better than we are. The new knowledge which science has acquired for us not only makes the muscles of our arms redundant, it is going to make many of those other faculties which we have prized seem almost second-place.' ('Science and the Christian', pp. 13f.)

Such has been the development in computers since Coulson wrote these words that even in a more complex game such as chess small microcomputers can now beat 99.5% of their human opponents.

In 1842 Lady Lovelace (Lord Byron's daughter) said about Babbage's Analytical Engine (the forerunner of the computer), 'It has no pretensions whatever to originate anything. It can only do what we know how to order it to perform.' This is not the case with some modern computers, which learn and remember as well as perform tasks independent of human instruction. This was a point that Coulson made in his fourth Freemantle Lecture delivered at Balliol College, Oxford, in 1968.

10. On this see especially J. Weizenbaum, *Computer Power and Human Reason: From Judgment to Calculation*, W. H. Freeman 1976.

11. In Vonnegut's *Sirens of Titan*, Dell 1959, pp. 274–5, there appears the following legend which is told by a sentient machine to explain how its planet of Tralfamadore is now inhabited solely by machines like itself:

> Once upon a time on Tralfamadore there were creatures who weren't anything like machines. They weren't dependable. They weren't efficient. They weren't predictable. They weren't durable. And these poor creatures were obsessed with the idea that everything that existed had to have a purpose, and that some purposes were higher than others.
>
> These creatures spent most of their time trying to find out what their purpose was. And everytime they found out what seemed to be a purpose of themselves, the purpose seemed so low that the creatures were filled with disgust and shame.
>
> And, rather than serve such a low purpose, the creatures would make a machine to serve it. This left the creatures free to serve higher purposes. But whenever they found a higher purpose, the purpose still wasn't high enough.
>
> So machines were made to serve higher purposes, too. And the machines did everything so expertly that they were finally given the job of finding out what the highest purpose of the creatures could be.
>
> The machines reported in all honesty that the creatures couldn't really be said to have any purpose at all.
>
> The creatures thereupon began slaying each other, because they hated purposeless things above all else.
>
> And they discovered they weren't even very good at slaying. So they turned that job over to the machines, too. And the machines finished up the job in less time than it takes to say 'Tralfamadore'.

12. Quoted by Coulson in *SCB*, p. 5.

13. Coulson himself falls into this category. He was an expert on the properties of graphite, and during and after the Second World War he was asked to contribute his expertise to atomic bomb research, but he refused.

14. *SRS*, p. 15.

15. 'Science touches politics because science can provide what we could call a cohesive force within society and between societies', second Pegram Lecture, p. 16.

16. Richard Rhodes, *The Making of the Atomic Bomb*, Simon and Schuster 1986.

17. Despite its great size (886 pages) and occasional arcane descriptions of scientific processes, Rhodes' book makes for compelling reading. The actual making of the bomb is not described until the second half of the book, and the first half details the important events which lead up to the discovery of nuclear fission. We are also offered biographical sketches of the scientists involved and analysis of the social and political situations in which they lived and worked. It is towards the end of the book that it becomes apparent why Rhodes situates the making of the bomb in this larger context: he is writing more than a history of the bomb, he is writing a defence of science itself.

18. 'Science and the Christian', lecture 2, p. 6.

19. Rhodes, op. cit., p. 783.
20. Rhodes, op. cit., p. 785.

5 Responsibility in a Scientific Age

1. The fourth Pegram Lecture on 'Science and Human Responsibility', p. 5.
2. 'Commitment', p. 28.
3. *STC*, p. 75.
4. *STC*, pp. 15–16. See also *Nuclear Knowledge*, p. 8: 'If we believe that it is God's will that his children everywhere should enjoy the benefits of civilization, then we are committed to a fair and reasonable distribution of the economic benefits of atomic energy. To say that God is not concerned with these things is to emasculate the Christian life of its goodness; it is to cloud over the vision of men like Scott Holland and our own Scott Lidgett; it is to deny God's beneficence in making this fuller life possible; it is to reject the worthwhileness of the material world, and to retreat to a pietism more Buddhist than Christian.'
One wonders, however, whether Coulson would have continued to support a way of producing power which we now know to be hazardous after the accidents at Three Mile Island and Chernobyl, and after the fuller information which has now come to light about the Windscale disaster. See, for example, Coulson's comments about the need to be acquainted with all the facts in *PAA*, p. 24–8.
5. 'Commitment', p. 36.
6. Alan Russell and Norris D. McWhirter (eds), *The Guinness Book of Records*, Guinness Books 1988, p. 187.
7. It is quite probable, however, that the passage of time may well have tempered Coulson's enthusiasm for certain methods of birth control had he lived to see some of the evidence which has accumulated to show that the Pill and the IUD are not without detrimental effects.
8. For example, in an address entitled 'Technology and Humanity' delivered at a study week held in 1972, Coulson called for more environmental concern, a new economics of stationary equilibrium, a global study of resources, the abolition of the profit motive or at least the 'sublimation' of it, and a new attitude to work. As early as 1932 he had publicly allied himself with the Peace Movement, and endorsed the statement of the Cambridge Scientists' Anti-War Group founded in 1933 which called for co-operation with the working class (because they suffered most in war) and in the event of war a possible strike against the transport of munitions.
9. *STC*, ch. 5.
10. 'Commitment', p. 40.
11. *SCT*, p. 7.
12. *Responsibility*, p. 12.
13. Ibid., p. 13. To this list could be added Niels Bohr and Leo Szilard. Both of these eminent physicists worked tirelessly to convince the Allies that unleashing the power of the atom demanded international co-operation and responsibility – see Rhodes, op. cit. On the other hand, it must be said that there are scientists who display no such concern – see W. Broad, *Starwarriors: A Penetrating Look into the Lives of the Young Scientists behind our Space Age*

Weaponry, Simon and Schuster 1985. We should also note that Tartaglia changed his mind when war threatened to overtake his own government, and divulged the secrets of his experiments in gunnery – a good example of the difficult choices scientists sometimes have to make.

14. Hans Jonas, *The Imperative of Responsibility: In Search of an Ethics for the Technological Age*, University of Chicago Press 1984, p. x.

15. Ibid., p. 45.

16. *PAA*, 15–16.

17. 'Commitment', p. 54: 'But this is not just a scientific or just a political response [to the developing countries], for it is bound up with our very nature as human beings. So in a recent issue of the scientific journal, *Nature*, the editor ponders on these things. In effect he says: "Whether the underdeveloped parts of the world will or will not achieve the standard of living that they seek will not depend solely on the provision of a suitable number of technologists, engineers, teachers and the like, it will depend on whether we have a worthy view of man."'

18. *PAA*, p. 35.

19. *PAA*, p. 38.

20. *Responsibility*, p. 2.

21. Cf. *Nuclear Knowledge* p. 15: 'A worthy view of man is possible only by the side of a worthy view of God.'

22. Quoted by Coulson in *STC*, p. 55.

23. *PAA*, p. 21.

24. *Responsibility*, p. 23.

25. Ibid. Coulson was indebted to Rosenstock-Huessy for this idea – see *SCB*, p. 106.

26. The third Sir Owen Evans Lecture on 'The World of People – Redeption', p. 3.

27. Ibid., p. 8: 'The slogan of one of the parties was, "You've never had it so good" – you remember it, I'm sure. But not to be outdone in this charitable view of life, the other main rival party effectively chose for its slogan, "If you vote for us, you'll have it better." I longed that those who see things as I think a Christian should see them would get up and say, "A plague on both of your houses!" This is no way for a community to act responsibly . . .'

28. Cf. *PAA*, p. 8: 'If the magnificent and splendid opportunities with which this new Atomic Age presents us are to be grasped, it will be because people like ourselves have been clear-headed enough, and sufficiently imaginative to interpret the mind of Christ with these new and strangely unfamiliar conditions.'

29. Cf. *STC*, p. 108f.: 'It is for the Christian to set the pattern of thought against which decisions and action may be judged. The Christian really is the leaven in the lump. Only those who know the inner nature of Man, and the peculiar ways in which God transforms a man's mind by the renewing power of his Spirit, and the status that God confers on him that he may be called a child of God, are big enough to speak to the condition of today. Scientists cannot think out their problems alone . . . Nor can politicians achieve the ends that they desire, despite their claim that "politics is the art of getting things done", without the appropriate climate of opinion. This

climate they are almost completely powerless to create. Yet it is one of the greatest contributions that Christian people can make, if they bestir themselves.'

6   Coulson in the Contemporary Context

1. Letter to 'Ernest', 30 June 1930. This is one of a number of letters which, together with other material relating to the activities of the Methodist Group Movement, is found among a collection of papers in Wesley House, Cambridge.

2. Cf. S. L. Altmann and E. J. Bowen in the *Memoir*, op. cit., p. 77: 'From then on [after his "spiritual renewal"] his Christian faith was the driving force in his life and he knew he would dedicate his life to religion, by which he meant science and everything else as well. This was a great intellectual leap at the time: in the Cambridge of the 1920s the divorce between science and religion was almost absolute.'

3. Cupitt, *The Words of Science and Religion*, p. 33.

4. Quoted by S. Andrews, 'Methodism and Science', *Epworth Review* 14, 1987, p. 33.

5. Ibid.

6. Thomas Beyes, *Divine Benevolence or an Attempt to prove that the Principal End of the Divine Providence and Governance is the Happiness of His Creatures*, John Noone 1731. I am grateful to my friend Richard Gaffney for drawing my attention to this reference. This is the same Thomas Beyes who is well known to statisticians.

7. 'A Secular World? God and Things', *Laity* 16, 1963, p. 31.

8. Coulson notes how in Job 38 the morning stars sing together for joy at creation's birth, and also how the words of St Francis' hymn of praise, 'All creatures of our God and King', have the whole of creation praising God.

9. 'A Scientist's View of the Honest to God Debate', *Impetus* 3, 1966, p. 34.

10. 'The Methodist Doctrine of Perfect Love', *Proceedings of the Tenth World Methodist Conference* ed. E. Benson Perkins and Elmer T. Clark, Epworth Press 1961, p. 284.

11. Cited in John A. Newton, *A Man for all Churches: Marcus Ward*, Epworth Press 1984, p. 34.

12. Found in the Wesley House Collection of Papers and dated 21 December 1932.

13. In a letter found in the Wesley House Collection and dated 30 March 1936, Coulson speaks of building up a 'kind of synthesis of souls and bodies' and adds impishly, 'a kind of lesserweatherheading'.

14. 'The Earth is the Lord's', *Christian Education* 21, 1962, p. 50.

15. *SRS*, p. 21.

16. In his inaugural lecture at Oxford in 1952, published as *The Spirit of Applied Mathematics*, Clarendon Press 1953, Coulson stressed the impossibility of knowing exactly where science may lead. Often theories in 'pure mathematics' which would seem to have no possible practical application can become very significant in applied mathematics. It was A. N. Whitehead who had quite correctly drawn attention to the impressive way in which 'as mathematics withdrew increasingly into the upper regions of ever

greater extremes of abstract thought, it returned back to earth with a corresponding growth of importance for the analysis of concrete fact.' (p. 8)

17. See Julian Huxley et al., *Science and Religion: A Symposium*, Gerald Howe 1931, pp. 93ff.

18. William Murray, 'Genetic Engineering: Brave New Science', *Cosmopolitan* June 1975, p. 187.

19. *Time*, 30 October 1980. p. 68.

20. We should perhaps note that Coulson himself did not object in principle to cloning – see *SRS*, p. 21.

21. *SCB*, p. 88.

22. A recording of this lecture is kept among Coulson's papers at the Bodleian Library in Oxford.

23. Jonas, *The Imperative of Responsibility*, p. 45.

24. See K. Temple, '"No Nukes" is Not Enough', *Research in Philosophy and Technology* 6, 1983, pp. 189–97.

25. Nor, we might add, is it a coincidence that both of these philosophies became linked with fascism.

26. Indeed, in a contribution to a symposium on the morality of atomic warfare Coulson spoke of *philosophy* being discredited – see *Atomic Scientists Journal* 4, 1954, p. 10.

27. Martin Luther, 'An Open Letter on the Harsh Book Against the Peasants' (1525), *Luther's Works* 6, Philadelphia 1967, pp. 69f.

Appendix A

1. In particular the advent of space technology has given us new information and insights – see M. S. Longair, 'Space Science and Cosmology', in *Understanding the Universe: The Impact of Space Astronomy* ed. Richard M. West, D. Reidel Publishing Company 1983, pp. 129–225.

2. The sheer size of the universe raises one especially interesting theological question. It has been speculated that in such a vast universe other 'earths' are possible with life like our own. Is, therefore, the revelation which we have in Christ for them also, or will each of these other earths have its own revelation? The question, in other words, is about the particularity of the Christian revelation in the kind of universe the scientists have shown us. On how this also involves our understanding of personhood, see Ernan McMullin, 'Persons in the Universe', *Zygon* 15, 1980, pp. 69–89.

3. This is the account Coulson gave of the incident in the unpublished typescript of his Sir D. Owen Evans Lectures, 'The Influence of Science on Christian Faith', given in 1966 at the University of Aberystwyth: 'The University of Oxford acted as hosts to a deputation from the University of Moscow. The group who came were of course very safe communists – otherwise they wouldn't have been in that party. When they came, in order to show them the typical ordinary life of the university, we put on all sorts of special shows! One of these was an address by myself on the influence of the churches on religious life in Britain. It very much surprised our communist friends that it should be a professional scientist who would be speaking about the role of the churches. When I had finished and the chairman asked for questions, it was not long before one of the party, himself a professional physicist in Moscow, got up and said, Yes, there was one question he would

like to ask me. He was a bit surprised that someone whom he understood to be a professional scientist should have been speaking as I had spoken. He wondered if I accepted the view, which he accepted (and which I hastened to say I did too), that the age of this earth was in the order of 5,000 million years and that the age of human life was perhaps 5 million and responsible human life only a tenth of that, if that much, which corresponded to about one minute out of a day. So, he said, if you believe that, aren't you asking me to believe something very strange about what you call God? Isn't he a pretty inefficient workman if it took him all that time before the human race came? You have been saying that you must think of him in terms of fatherhood and love, yet that only began to have meaning one minute ago out of the day!

Well, of course, he was right. I don't know what you would have said if you had been placed in the position in which I was placed. But what I said was that the only way to make sense out of the huge scale of unrecorded time is to suppose that in some sense God found fulfilment and some interest in it.'

4. Polkinghorne, *One World*, p. 57.

5. The speed of a receding galaxy has to be adduced by indirect evidence. This is done through studying the so-called Doppler effect, which says that if a source of waves, such as light or sound, is moving away from us, the frequency which we ourselves receive and measure is less than if the source had been at rest. There is an everyday example which illustrates the point in the case of sound. If a car passes us the pitch of the noise drops as it moves away from us. In the case of light colour is shifted towards the red end of the spectrum. The speed of the source of light can be worked out by measuring this red shift. It was Hubble and Humason who, through calculations based on the Doppler effect, concluded that the speed of recession of a nebula is directly proportional to its distance from us. This became known as the Hubble–Humason law.

6. Another useful anology is that of the currant pudding which expands when baked in the oven. As it expands the currants move further apart. Unlike that of the balloon, this analogy is three-dimensional.

7. It is perhaps of interest to note here that one of Coulson's mentors, Arthur Eddington, did not believe that the universe originated in a big bang. For him the beginning of the universe was more like a whimper. An original volume of space, filled with a fog-like matter, broke up into conglomerations of matter which became galaxies and began moving away from each other. No big bang here!

8. Fred Hoyle, *The Nature of the Universe*, Blackwell 1950.

9. The phenomenon of supercooling can be observed in water. Under normal conditions water will change to ice at 0°C, but when supercooled it changes to ice at −20°C.

10. There is a simplified account in A. H. Guth and P. J. Steinhardt, 'The Inflationary Universe', *Scientific American*, May 1984, p. 90.

11. See Polkinghorne, *One World*, pp. 56–9.

12. See John D. Barrow and Frank J. Tipler, *The Anthropic Cosmological Principle*, Clarendon Press 1986.

13. P. C. W. Davies, *The Accidental Universe*, Cambridge University Press 1982, pp. 115f.

14. Some people think that we will have crossed the boundary from physics to metaphysics when (and if) physicists manage to formulate a 'theory of everything' (TOE) or a 'grand unified theory' (GUT). There are two fundamental frameworks used by present day physicists. One is Einstein's theory of gravity (general relativity) which explains the behaviour of large objects such as planets and stars, and the other is quantum mechanics which is used in the understanding of the sub-atomic world. The two seem to operate on different principles and there is a fundamental problem in reconciling them. The quest for a GUT is an attempt to reconcile them and thus all laws of physics in one unified theory. The latest contenders for this holy grail of physics are Michael Green, John H. Schwartz and Edward Whitten, who have recently published their ideas in *Superstring Theory* (2 vols.), Cambridge University Press 1987. The basic idea is that at the ultimate sub-atomic level there are no 'points' or particles, but rather matter is 'strung out' in the manner of strings. In superstring theory our concepts of time and space are radically changed, for strings exist in a ten dimensional universe. This may well have metaphysical implications, but it is difficult to tell at this stage what they may be.

Appendix B

1. Jonathan Schell, *The Fate of the Earth*, Cape 1982.

2. Statement contributed to Symposium on the Morality of Atomic Warfare in *Atomic Scientists Journal* 4, 1954, p. 10.

3. 'Science and Pacifism', address given to Methodist Peace Fellowship, Oxford, 1969, p. 10f. (Unpublished MS found among Coulson's papers in the Bodleian Library.)

4. Ibid., pp. 12f.

5. Ibid., p. 11.

Bibliography

Alexander, P., Review of *Science and Christian Belief*, *British Journal of the Philosophy of Science*, 8, 1958, pp. 76–8

Altmann, S. L. and E. J. Bowen, 'Charles Alfred Coulson', *Biographical Memoirs of the Royal Society* 20, 1974, pp. 75–114

Andrews, S., 'Methodism and Science', *Epworth Review* 14, 1987, pp. 32–9

Barrow, J. D. and F. J. Tipler, *The Anthropic Cosmological Principle*, Clarendon Press 1986

Bartholomew, D. J., *God of Chance*, SCM Press 1984

Bevan, R. J. W., *Steps to Christian Understanding*, Oxford University Press 1958

Beyes, T., *Divine Benevolence or an Attempt to Prove that the Principal End of the Divine Providence and Governance is the Happiness of His Creatures*, John Noone 1731

Boslough, J., *Beyond the Black Hole: Stephen Hawking's Universe*, Collins 1985

Broad, W., *Starwarriors: A Penetrating Look into the Lives of the Young Scientists behind our Space Age Weaponry*, Simon and Schuster 1985

Broom, D. M., *Biology of Behaviour: Mechanisms, Functions and Applications*, Cambridge University Press 1981

Bultmann, R., *Jesus Christ and Mythology*, Scribner 1958 and SCM Press 1960

Cupitt, D., *The Worlds of Science and Religion*, Sheldon Press 1976

Darwin, C., *On the Origin of Species by Natural Selection*, John Murray 1859

Davies, P. C. W., *The Accidental Universe*, Cambridge University Press 1982

——, *The Cosmic Blueprint*, Heinemann 1987

Davies, R. (ed), *An Approach to Christian Education*, Epworth Press 1956

Dawkins, R., *The Blind Watchmaker*, Longman 1986 and Penguin Books 1988

Dyson, F., *Disturbing the Universe*, Harper and Row 1979

Dyson-Hudson, R. and M. A. Little, *Rethinking Human Adaptation*, Bowker 1983

Eddington, A. S., *Science and the Unseen World*, Allen and Unwin 1929

Feyerabend, P., *Against Method*, Verse 1975

Grant, G. P., *Philosophy in the Mass Age*, Copp Clark 1966

——, *Technology and Empire*, House of Anansi 1969

——, *Technology and Justice*, University of Notre Dame Press 1986

Guth, A. H. and P. J. Steinhardt, 'The Inflationary Universe', *Scientific American*, May 1984, pp. 90ff.

Hawking, S. W., *A Brief History of Time*, Bantam Books 1988

Hesse, M., *Revolutions and Reconstructions in the Philosophy of Science*, The Harvester Press 1980

Hoyle, F., *The Nature of the Universe*, Blackwell 1950

——, *The Intelligent Universe*, Michael Joseph 1983

Huxley, Julian et al., *Science and Religion: A Symposium*, Gerald Howe 1931

Jantzen, G. M., *God's World, God's Body*, Darton, Longman and Todd 1984

Jeans, J., *The Mysterious Universe*, Cambridge University Press 1931

Jonas, H., *The Imperative of Responsibility: In Search of an Ethics for the Technological Age*, University of Chicago Press 1984

Kitcher, P., *Vaulting Ambition: Sociobiology and the Quest for Human Nature*, MIT 1985

Koestler, A. *Heel of Achilles: Essays 1968–78*, Picador 1976

——, *Arrival and Departure*, Hutchinson 1966

Kohák, E., *The Embers and the Stars: A Philosophical Inquiry into the Moral Sense of Nature*, University of Chicago Press 1984

Koyré, A., *From Closed World to Infinite Universe*, John Hopkins Press 1957

Kuhn, T., *The Structure of Scientific Revolutions*, University of Chicago Press 1962, second and revised edition 1970

Lack, D., *Evolutionary Theory and Christian Belief*, Methuen 1957

Lonergan, B. J. F., *Insight: A Study of Human Understanding*, Longman 1957

Lumsden, C. J. and E. O. Wilson, *Genes, Mind and Culture: The Co-evolutionary Process*, Harvard University Press 1981

Margenau, H., *The Nature of Physical Reality*, McGraw-Hill 1950
McMullin, E., 'Persons in the Universe', *Zygon* 15, 1980, pp. 69–89
Monod, J., *Chance and Necessity*, Collins 1972
Morris, D., *The Naked Ape: A Zoologist's Study of the Human Animal*, Cape and McGraw-Hill 1967
Montefiore, H., *The Probability of God*, SCM Press 1985
Newton, J. A., *A Man for all Churches: Marcus Ward*, Epworth Press 1984
Newton-Smith, W. H., *The Rationality of Science*, Routledge and Kegan Paul 1981
Nouy, P. Lecomte du, *Human Destiny*, Longman 1947
Oakley, D. A. and H. C. Plotkin, *Brain Behaviour and Evolution*, Methuen 1979
Peacocke, A., *Science and the Christian Experiment*, Oxford University Press 1971
——, *Creation and the World of Science*, Clarendon Press 1979
——, *God and the New Biology*, Dent 1986
Polanyi, M., *Science, Faith and Society*, Oxford University Press 1946
Polkinghorne, J., *One World: The Interaction of Science and Theology*, SPCK 1986
——, *The Quantum World*, Penguin Books 1986
Pollard, W. G., *Chance and Providence*, Scribner 1958
Raven, C., *Experience and Interpretation*, Cambridge University Press 1953
Rhodes, R., *The Making of the Atomic Bomb*, Simon and Schuster 1986
Smith, J. Maynard (ed), *Evolution Now: A Century after Darwin*, *Nature* in association with Macmillan 1982
Teilhard de Chardin, P., *The Phenomenon of Man*, Collins 1959
Temple, K. '"No Nukes" is not enough', *Research in Philosophy and Technology* 6, 1983, pp. 189–97
Tsuang, Ming T. and R. Vandermay, *Genes and the Mind: Inheritance of Mental Illness*, Oxford University Press 1980
Vonnegut, K., *Sirens of Titan*, Dell 1959
Waddington, C. H., *The Ethical Animal*, Allen and Unwin 1960
Watson, James D., *The Double Helix*, Weidenfeld and Nicolson 1968
Weizenbaum, J., *Computer Power and Human Reason: From Judgement to Calculation*, W. H. Freeman 1976
West, R. M. (ed), *Understanding the Universe: The Impact of Space Astronomy*, D. Reidel Publishing Company 1983
Whitehouse, W. A., *Christian Faith and the Scientific Attitude*, Oliver and Boyd 1952

Wilberforce, S., *Essays Contributed to the Quarterly Review*, London 1874

Wiles, M., *God's Action in the World*, SCM Press 1986

Wilson, E. O., *Sociobiology: The New Synthesis*, Harvard University Press 1975

——, *On Human Nature*, Harvard University Press 1978

Index

Adam, 13, 20, 79, 113n
Altmann, S. L., 107n, 111n, 117n, 121
Anthropic cosmological principle, 89f.
Aristotle, 7, 28
Augustine, 9, 80, 95, 107n

Bacon, Roger, 53
Balguy, John, 78
Barrow, John, D., 119n, 121
Bartholomew, David J., 31, 110n, 121
Beales, Harold, 2
Beyes, Thomas, 79, 117n, 121
Big bang theory, 88ff., 119n
Birth control, 67, 115n
Bohr, Niels, 42, 47, 115n
Bomb, atomic, 35, 41, 51, 59f., 81f., 95, 96, 123
Bowen, E. J., 107n, 111n, 117n, 121
Boyle, Robert, 24, 69
Bragg, Sir Lawrence, 45
Bridgeman, Percy, 62
Burnet, MacFarland, 20
Burrett, Eileen, 3
Burt, Sir Cyril, 43

Chernobyl, 115n
Cherwell, Lord, 58, 100
Complementarity, principle of, 42
Compton, Arthur, 35

Conant, J. B., 38, 70
Constantine, 94
Continuous creation, 89
Copernicus, Nicholas, 7, 8, 90
Cosmology, 7ff., 77, 87
Creation, 7ff., 22, 73, 77, 79, 88ff.
Cuckoo, 31, 32, 110n
Cunningham, E., 2
Cupitt, Don, 77, 110n, 112n, 117n, 121

da Vinci, Leonardo, 69
Darwin, Charles, 16, 20, 25, 100, 109n, 112n, 121
Davies, P. C. W., 89, 98, 119n, 121
Dawkins, Richard, 32, 110n, 122
Descartes, R., 26, 73
Design, argument from, 31f.
Dewey, John, 40
Doppler effect, 119n
Drummond, Henry, 27
du Nouy, Lecomte, P., 18, 19, 24, 108n, 123

Ecology, 73, 74
Eddington, A. S., 2, 24, 33, 34, 88, 119n, 122
Einstein, Albert, 8, 13, 14, 28, 36, 60, 108n, 120n
Electron, 28, 30, 41, 42

Evans, Sir D. Owen, 18, 103, 109n, 116n, 118n
Evolution, 12, 15ff., 22, 25, 47, 88, 90

Fairy shrimp, 19
Faraday, Michael, 26, 33, 60, 110n
Forster, E. M., 52

Galileo, 7ff., 42, 52f.
Genesis, 12ff., 17, 73, 90
Genetic engineering, 20, 26, 82ff., 118n
Gandhi, 64
Gilliam, T., 52
Gissing, George, 71
God of the Gaps, 27, 32
Grand unified theory, 120n
Grant, George, 50, 112n, 122
Gregory, Sir Richard, 25
Guth, Alan, 89, 119n, 122

Hardy, G. H., 2
Hawking, Stephen, 47, 109n, 121, 122
Heidegger, M., 84
Heinemann, F. H., 73, 121
Heisenberg, Werner von, 27, 30, 47
Heisenberg's Uncertainty Principle, 27ff.,
Hippocratic Oath, 72
Hiroshima, 51, 102
Hooker, Joseph, 16
Hoyle, Fred, 18, 47, 89, 108n, 119n, 122
Hubble-Humason law, 119n
Huxley, Aldous, 40
Huxley, Julian, 118n
Huxley, T. H., 16, 36

Idealism, 37
Incarnation, 10, 48, 79, 85

Jeans, James, 17, 33, 122
Jonas, Hans, 69, 70, 84, 116n, 122

Kellaway, Ernest, 40
Kennedy, President John, 57
Kepler, Johannes, 7
Kingsley, Charles, 18
Koestler, Arthur, 54, 112n, 113n, 122
Kohák, Erazim, 48, 112n, 122

Lack, David, 58, 102, 108n, 122
Lang, F., 52
Le Maître, 88
Lea, Douglas, 2
Lennard-Jones, J. E., 2
Luther, Martin, 7, 85, 101, 118n

Marxism, 85
Maxwell, C., 36
McMullin, Ernan, 118n, 123
McNair, John Calvin, 23, 97, 103, 109n
Method, scientific, 33ff., 53
Methodism, 5, 77, 80, 117n, 121
Methodist 'Groups', 2, 80, 81, 107n, 117n
Methodist Peace Fellowship, 92
Monod, Jacques, 31, 110n, 123
Montefiore, Hugh, 76, 77, 110n, 123
Murray, William, 83, 118n

Nation-state, 56, 58, 60, 61
Newton, Isaac, 8, 24, 26, 27, 53

Oppenheimer, J. Robert, 81
Otto, Rudolph, 13, 51, 71, 81
Overpopulation, 64, 66
Oxfam, 5, 64, 65, 70, 94

Pacifism, 92ff., 109n
Pain, problem of, 48

Paley, William, 32
Peacocke, Arthur, 24, 45, 46,
    112n, 123
Perfectionism, 80
Pietism, 80, 115n
Planck, Max, 35
Polanyi, M., 38, 102, 123
Polkinghorne, John, 24, 28, 36–
    38, 88, 110n, 119n, 123
Pollard, W. G., 29, 30, 110n, 123
Positivism, 37
Ptolemy, 7

Quantum theory, 3, 27ff., 55,
    120n

Raven, Charles, 16, 98, 102,
    110n, 123
Ray, John, 24, 46, 112n
Realist, critical, 37
Reductionism, 38ff., 53, 78,
    111n
Reflection, act of, 40, 46, 82
Religious activity, science as a,
    23, 24, 43ff., 70, 71, 78, 85, 93
Responsibility, 13, 17, 61ff.,
    68ff., 80ff.
Rhodes, Richard, 59ff., 114n,
    115n, 123
Roosevelt, President Franklin,
    42
Royal Society, 4, 5, 24, 51, 56,
    59, 107n, 121
Rutherford, Ernest, 2, 60, 63

Sagan, Carl, 83, 93
Sarton, G., 38
Schell, J., 93, 120n
Schroedinger, Erwin, 72, 101
Sociobiology, 111n, 112n
Spencer, Herbert, 72

Streeter, B. H., 82
Super-cooling, 89
Superposition, 28
Superstring theory, 120n

Tartaglia, 69, 116n
Teilhard de Chardin, P., 18, 19,
    31, 121
Temple, K., 118n, 123
Theology, natural, 31ff., 53
Thompson, J. J., 2, 51, 52, 60
Three Mile Island, 115n
Tipler, Frank J., 119n, 121
Trinity College, Cambridge, 2,
    3, 26

Ussher, James, 9, 107n

Vonnegut, K., 52, 55, 114n,
    123

Waddington, C. H., 25, 49,
    112n, 123
Wallis, John, 24
Ward, Marcus, 80, 117n, 123
Weiszaecker, Carl F. von, 47
Wesley, John, 77, 85, 112n
Whewell, William, 52
Whitehead, A. N., 38, 117n
Whitehouse, W. A., 29, 110n,
    123
Wilberforce, S., 16, 17, 25,
    108n, 123
Wilkens, John, 24
Windscale, 115n
Winter, nuclear, 61, 93
Wood, Alex, 44, 97
World Council of Churches, 5
Wren, Christopher, 24

Zamyatin, I., 52